Bow Before the Mystery that Remains

Bow Before the Mystery that Remains

A Journey Toward Recovery from Grief and Trauma

Kathleen Shelby Boyett
(with Vera Nooner)

Searching Mink Publishing
Charlotte, North Carolina

Unless otherwise noted, Scriptures are taken from the Holy Bible, New International Version®, NIV®. Copyright © 1973, 1978, 1984, 2011 by Biblica, Inc.™ Used by permission of Zondervan.

Holy Bible, New Living Translation, Copyright © 1996, 2004, 2015 by Tyndale House Foundation. Used by permission of Tyndale House Publishers, Inc., Carol Stream, Illinois 60188. All rights reserved.

Copyright © 2023 Kathleen Shelby Boyett
ISBN: 9798393701642

All rights reserved. No part of this publication may be reproduced, distributed, or transmitted in any form or by any means, including photocopying, recording, or other electronic or mechanical methods, without the prior written permission of the publisher except for the use of brief quotations in a book review.

Contents

~~~~~~~~~~~~~~~~~~~~~~~~~

My Hopes for This Book
1

Explaining the Title of this Book
3

Introduction
5

Part I:
Grandmother Vera Nooner's Story
9

Part II:
Granddaughter Shelby Boyett's Story
87

Part III:
Discoveries
179

Part IV:
The Most Important Faith Lessons
199

Part V:
Helps for Coping with Grief and Loss
209

My Hopes for This Book

I have had the feeling that God was upholding me throughout this whole difficult time. Somehow I have continued on, despite the pain, and I know that I have not done this solely on my own. It is in times like this when you feel God's presence most. (Psalms 34:18 – "The Lord is near to the brokenhearted." He really is!) If you lean on Him, He will uphold you. I can say this with all confidence: God is real and He is there for you. Jesus is your true husband and He will never let you go. He will never let you slip out of His hand. (John 10:28 – "I give them eternal life, and they shall never perish; no one will snatch them out of my hand.")

I can only hope that someone reading these words will be helped and encouraged as they stand by their loved one with dementia or cancer.

I also hope that someone who is facing unusual behavior from their loved one will decide to check for dementia as a cause, even if that loved one is younger than when you would expect dementia to strike.

Perhaps this book can enable someone else to better understand the difficult behavior of a loved one who has already passed. It is never too late to gain more healing.

God be with you and may He hold you in the palm of His hand and comfort you – He can and will do it!

Explaining the Title of this Book

"You don't understand now what I am doing, but someday you will."
Jesus (in John 13:7)

When I decided to produce a second edition of the book, *Till Death Do Us Part*, I wanted to change the title. The previous title was chosen because it was what my grandmother wanted to use for the title of her short manuscript, had she ever been able to publish it, and I chose to honor that. Now that the story has expanded to include not only cancer and dementia, but also trauma and the effects of these on the human brain, I feel the story has become more truly mine. The new title describes very well the difficulty I have had in my journey to be satisfied with the answers that are available and not persist in trying to find the answers that will have to remain a mystery. We all must choose to bow before the wisdom of God in what He has decided to reveal and what He has decided to keep hidden.

Introduction

This book is not only a story I had to write for my own sake, but the fulfillment of something my Grandmother wanted to do – help others. I hope that my contributions to her story and adding my own story will accomplish the same thing: to give hope to someone who is hurting and mourning the loss of a loved one, either to death or to dementia – what I call "the grieving before the grieving" – and the resultant trauma.

Unfortunately, my story is somewhat harsher than the one my Grandmother told. I have chosen not to change any of the diary entries I quote nor any of the facts of what actually happened to my husband and me. Although our story is quite painful, it is a story someone else may be facing, and I want that person to understand the deep emotions that come with dementia and trauma and the suffering involved. I want them to know that what they are feeling is normal.

Then, I want the reader to see that there is hope! I

want you to know that you can come out of your deep sorrow enough to be victorious in the Lord, who can be your strength if you let Him. It's true that you will never be quite the same person you were before your trauma and loss. Yet, while you will never forget your loved one and the time you shared – and actually never completely stop grieving your loss – God can redeem the years lost to you in pain and grief.

Like Job in the Bible, you can receive more than was taken away from you: *a closer walk with God* – a walk that can sustain you through your trials and your pain. A walk with a God who will never leave you and can always be depended on. A walk with a God you can trust. And in the case of a woman who has lost her husband to death or to divorce, a God who is a new and perfect husband that will never betray you, or let you down, or stop loving you – or complain that you didn't wash the dishes! Your faith can become more resilient, more practically helpful every day, and more real to you as a result of your loss and trauma.

You can't just let the years go by and hope that time will do its job and heal you, however. Research has shown us that your loved one has actually imprinted upon your brain – you carry them with you always. You can use this fact to honor their memory, or to keep yourself stuck in grief. If you actively seek the Lord and His compassion, you can gain back some joy in your life. Spend as much time in His Word as you can. If it takes a while before you feel like reading scripture, that's OK and perfectly normal. Read a short devotional or even just one verse. Try the Psalms or the scriptures I have included in the back of this book. As time passes, you will feel more able to read and study the whole Word. As you learn more and more about God and how He cares for you, you will gain confidence to continue on with your life without your loved one.

Your life will not look or feel quite the same as before, and that's to be expected. You will, however, understand more and more how much God loves you and upholds you in trials and how His sovereignty assures that things will work out for your *ultimate* good ("And we know that God causes everything to work together for the good of those who love God and are called according to his purpose for them." Romans 8:28). After a while you will know beyond a shadow of a doubt that He has been the one who has sustained you through your grief and you will never again feel truly alone. His presence will be with you always and you will be able to FEEL it in a new way. ("Be renewed as you learn to know your Creator and become like Him." Colossians 3:10 NLT.)

This kind of new confidence doesn't happen overnight and you need to give yourself time to heal. Be kind to yourself and don't feel you have to rush. It will just gradually come upon you day by day, especially after the second year. Sometimes the second year of grief is harder than the first because the numbness that carried you through the first year has worn off. Don't let this throw you, just keep reading the Word and spend time in prayer.

Journaling can also be very helpful. Some journaling prompts are found in the last section of this book.

Try to notice something for which you can be grateful. Practicing gratitude is a wonderful way to feel better about things.

Another way to feel better is to help someone else. You will be surprised how being able to do even a small thing for someone will lift your mood.

God will honor your journey toward healing. Feel His loving arms wrap around you as you journey with my Grandmother and with me on our journeys to renewed joy.

PART I:

Vera Nooner's Story

Preston Christopher Nooner

Away

I cannot say, and I will not say
That he is dead. He is just away!

With a cheery smile, and a wave of the hand
He has wandered into an unknown land,

And left us dreaming how very fair
It needs must be, since he lingers there.

And you, O you, who the wildest yearn
For the old-time step and the glad return,

Think of him faring on, as dear
In the love of There as the love of Here.

Mild and gentle, as he was brave,
When the sweetest love of his life he gave

To simple things: Where the violets grew
Blue as the eyes they were likened to.

The touches of his hands have strayed
As reverently as his lips have prayed.

Think of him still as the same, I say:
He is not dead - he is just away!

James Whitcomb Riley
(slightly adapted)

Vera Nooner

Musings on the Brevity of Life
by Vera Nooner

Death is a work of nature.
It fulfils the purposes of nature.
Things change, persons die,
but the universe remains.

Everything lasts only for a day,
both that which remembers
and that which is remembered.

There is a continuous spinning of the threads and of the
single texture of the web.
Time is like a river made up of eventualities that happen.
The violent stream carries away the things that happened,
and another comes into place, only to be carried away too.

Sequences of things are fitted to those gone before.
You have to be like the cliff against which the waves
continually break.
It stands firm and tames the fury of the water around it.

So bear it nobly in good fortune. The interval between birth
and death is small.
Nothing happens to any man which he is not framed to
bear.

Think of the speed with which things pass and disappear.
Whatever is in any way beautiful, is beautiful in itself.

Preston and Vera in a moment of fun

P.C. with his daughters, Melba & Jean

Vera with a winsome smile

Daughter Melba, P.C., P.C.'s parents

P.C., Vera, daughter Jean

Vera and P.C.

P.C. relaxing with the newspaper

Shelby Boyett's Introduction

My grandfather, my mother's father, Preston Christopher Nooner, died at 7:15 a.m. on 17 March 1958 at San Augustine Hospital, in San Augustine, Texas. He was fifty-five years and twenty days old. I was a toddler of a year and a half.

His illness had been short, only lasting for three and a half months, from the day after Christmas in 1957 until his death in March. The diagnosis was a mouthful: glioblastoma multiforme of the left temporal lobe of brain. GBM is a highly malignant primary brain tumor.

The Mayo Clinic says that "Glioblastoma is an aggressive type of cancer that can occur in the brain or spinal cord. Glioblastoma forms from cells called astrocytes that support nerve cells. Glioblastoma can occur at any age, but tends to occur more often in older adults. It can cause worsening headaches, nausea, vomiting and seizures."

Naturally, some of the symptoms of GBM are caused by the increased pressure in the brain. My grandfather actually had a surgery in which a portion of his skull was removed so that the tumor could grow through the opening and cease to cause as much pain as he had been experiencing with the tumor pressing against his skull.

Even after all these years since my grandfather died, "Glioblastoma multiforme can be very difficult to treat and a cure is often not possible." The family knew from almost the beginning that there was no hope for his recovery.

My mother told me that the tumor was caused by a sinus surgery my grandfather had. Growing up, I knew none of the details of this surgery, or even if mother was correct about this being the cause of the tumor's formation. I do know that this idea stuck with her and she was vehemently opposed to anyone having a sinus surgery, but Grandmother's words here do not bear out that this was the cause.

On the 1930 census, P.C. Nooner was a head of household at age twenty-seven, with my grandmother, Vera Mae Hill Nooner, who was twenty-six, and my mother, who was two years old. This Census listed the person's age at their first marriage. P.C. was twenty-one and Vera was twenty when they were married on 10 January 1925 – exactly the same ages as my husband

and I were when we married in 1977.

The Nooners were renting their home for $15 a month in 1930. My grandfather's occupation was listed as a salesman in a drug store on this census: at San Augustine Drug, which was still there in my time. His occupation was given as a bookkeeper on my mother's birth certificate, and as a druggist on a 1954 copy of my mother's birth certificate, obviously filled out by the clerk with current information, not the information that was actually on the original certificate.

My grandfather worked long, hard hours at that job. My mother told me how he worked six days a week until 9.00 p.m. every night. He would come home for a quick evening meal, and go back to work for several hours. Then Sundays would also be full, often with visiting family in nearby Appleby, Texas, my grandmother's hometown. P.C. had little time to relax, or do anything for his own pleasure. Of course, much of his working life was during a very depressed economic time, and just to have work at all was nothing to take lightly.

The 19 April 1940 census found the Nooner family on "Center Highway" in San Augustine, and my aunt, Billie Jean, was on this census as an eight-year-old; my mother was twelve. P.C.'s occupation was given as "drug clerk" at a "retail drug store." He worked for fifty-two weeks, for

$1,360.00. In comparison: the Night Marshall, a city officer, made $1,050.00; an operating engineer on the pipe line made $2,000.00; a farmer made $260.00; a saleslady at a gift shop made $520.00; and a nurse made $104.00.

Of course, I don't remember my grandfather. He knew me well, however, and I have been told that Mother would place me on a blanket next to the couch where he was lying and that he took great joy in watching me play and toddle about.

A friend shared his memory of my grandfather: "Mr. P.C. Nooner was my Sunday School teacher in the Junior Sunday School Department at First Baptist Church. I remember Mr. Nooner as a soft-spoken, gentle, caring, loving man who enjoyed working with the youth." It is nice to know that my grandfather somehow found time to care for others outside his own family circle, and inspired a young man to still remember him.

When my grandmother wrote these words, she had no idea that her oldest granddaughter would go through a similar experience – similar due to cancer being the cause of my husband's death, but very different in some ways because my husband's personality so completely changed from the man he had once been. (My husband's story appears in Part II.)

Vera Nooner's Introduction

"He faded from the sunlight land of life – a victim of cancer."

Vera Nooner

It seemed necessary for me to write an account of this illness for two main reasons. First, because I find that in re-living the events I get an amount of release from tension and I also remember things that happened I had forgotten in the stress of grief that I was under. (So few people want to hear about it.)

Second, I feel that in putting these events on paper they may be a help to someone else, should they find themselves in the same situation.

During this illness I read any and everything I could find on this disease – which was not very much. It seemed if I could just talk to or read something that could shed some light on this disease, it would help a lot. Great is the courage and strength, both physical and mental, that it takes to go through such an ordeal. One needs to be strengthened from day to day. In the hope that someone will get courage and strength and maybe be able to do some little something for their loved one that they might not have thought of – a new way to show their love and devotion to one that is so precious to them as my husband was to me – I write of these events.

This is not written from a medical point of view, although the illness followed exactly the prognosis the doctors outlined at the time of the operation. It is rather the actions and reactions of the patient as observed by those who nursed and cared for him.

Some days I remember more vividly than others...

"I tried to be submissive to God's will – to be brave and strong. The harder I tried, the more God helped me."

Vera Nooner

A Diary of P.C. Nooner's Illness

(As told by Vera Nooner, with additions by Shelby Boyett,)

"*Surely goodness and mercy shall follow me all the days of my life*"   Psalm 23:6

Because P.C. believed in God and was led by him, surely – as sure as there is a God – all the goodness and mercy that God could give to him would be his. Day by day, his goodness and mercy would be given to P.C. as he needed it.

Christmas Day, 1957

All knew that P.C. was suffering from a terrific headache. All the force at the store [San Augustine Drug Store, where P.C. worked], and his family knew it, but since he had had bad headaches for years, no one thought anything about it at the time. We all knew that he had to take aspirin, Bufferin, and B.C. Powders for his headaches.

Christmas Day was spent with our families back home. Driving the distance of fifty miles in the morning and returning Christmas night.

P.C. told some of the family that day that he was going to a Doctor because something was bad wrong with his head.

Sunday, December 29, 1957

He worked December 26th and 27th and on the afternoon of the 26th, he went to a Dr. He had a physical examination with several tests being made. The significant thing about the examination revealed that he was unable to tell the Dr. his age. He worked on the 27th, not telling anyone anything about his visit to the Dr.

He came home at 8 p.m. on the night of the 29th and seemingly enjoyed his evening meal of turkey and dressing left over from Christmas. [His regular schedule was to work during the day, then come home for dinner in the early evening and then go back to work until 9 p.m.]

At the table he started crying and told me that something was bad wrong with him because people he had known all his life, he was unable to call their name. He said that he was losing his mind and you could tell he was distressed. I tried to tell him that things of that sort happen to all people at times, but he insisted this was different.

He left the table and took his bath, as was his custom, before lying down and looking at T.V. and resting. As he walked into the bedroom where the T.V. was, he told me I would have to cut the T.V. off because he could see four or five of everything. I cut the T.V. off and before I could cross the room, he was violently sick, vomiting and upset stomach. He had a bad cold. All night he was real sick. We hated to call a Dr. in the night, thinking he would be alright soon, but when daylight finally came, I called the Dr. he had gone to, the one he told me to call.

Monday, December 30, 1957

After a careful examination by the Dr., he diagnosed the illness as "nervous exhaustion" and started giving him tranquilizers. Under the sedation he began to talk about things we could not understand. For instance, he talked about "The Battery." My sister and myself tried every way we knew to find out what he meant, but he would finally laugh and say, "Forget it."

For the next three days, most of his talking was not coherent but he talked a great deal. He ate very little. He was able to go to the bathroom without our help. We had our good night prayer together and we would recite the Lord's Prayer and the 23rd Psalm.

The nights were not so good. He slept only a few minutes at a time. He seemed to have so much pain in his head, he could not lie down, so he would get up and sit in a chair. I thought that the fact that he Dr. had told him to quit smoking cigarettes was the main reason for his not being able to sleep, so I would fix him something to eat. This happened about every two hours. I would fix him ice cream, hot coco milk, sometimes an egg, tea tomato juice, orange juice, something different each time.

The latter part of this first week, he was able to go to the table, but had trouble getting food to his mouth and could hardly pick up a glass of milk. We put the card table in front of the picture window in the den and let him eat there so he could see people passing but he showed little interest in anything. He would go back to bed, then get up again in a few minutes. He was able to put on his house slippers and robe by himself and go to the bathroom alone.

Sunday, January 5, 1958

The Dr. told us to take him for a drive. His family came in the early p.m. and he sat in the living room with them. About 4 p.m. we put his top coat over his pajamas and carried him for a drive. We passed our house to see if he recognized it and he did – said he was not ready to go home yet and for our daughter, Melba, to drive on and he would give her instructions where to go. It was through town and to his rent houses in the colored section of town. He told her every corner to turn and the streets to go on and after seeing the houses, he directed the way home. When we got home, he went back to bed and never seemed so well again.

Monday, January 6

P.C. seemed to not feel so well and about the

middle of the morning started propulsion vomiting again. By afternoon he felt better but did not get up, and when the Dr. came in the late afternoon and saw he had had a set back and that there was a little paralysis on his right side. You could tell it only his mouth being slightly drawn.

The Dr. told us that he thought we should take him to a hospital where an arteriogram test could be made and insisted he be taken as soon as possible – the next morning, in fact.

All arrangements were made, a Dr. at the Liters Harris Clinic in Galveston was called and he secured a room at John Sealy Hospital in Galveston. [For more than a century, the University of Texas Medical Branch (UTMB Health) has served the needs of Texas and Texans from its large Galveston campus. John Sealy Hospital opened on January 10, 1890, with 108 ward beds. When the University of Texas Medical Branch opened in October 1891, John Sealy Hospital became its primary teaching facility.]

P.C. was real nervous and seemed to know something unusual was happening even though we tried to keep it from him.

Tuesday, January 7

We left by ambulance at 8 a.m. on the eleventh day of his illness. I put a blanket over him in the ambulance. He had an excruciating headache – the only intense pain he suffered during the eighty days. (In later notes, Vera added: The brain controls pain in the body, but has no sensory nerves in brain tissue itself. The headache was caused from pressure on the brain tissue. In this case, it was the tumor that caused the pressure.)

We were checked in at John Sealy at 1 p.m. On the way, P.C. didn't talk and didn't seem to notice very much, just not interested but at the ferry at Port Boliver he said he would like a Coke. He drank it and seemed to enjoy it. I rode in the ambulance by him.

Shortly after arriving at John Sealy I was taken to a room away from P.C. and interviewed. Since P.C. couldn't talk, I had to give all the history of the case from which they were able to handle the case. The fact that he was unable to tell the Dr. at home his age was very significant to them and they used that fact for much of their diagnosis and worked on that fact a lot.

P.C. was placed in the neuro surgery ward where he was under observation at all times. A great number of tests were made including X-rays. The Drs. started at his waist line and examined every part of the body to the top of his head. The neurosurgeons questioned us at length about any chilly feelings, propulsion vomiting, double vision, dizziness, any change in taste, smell, hearing, any headaches, any changes in gait. As a matter of fact, P.C. had had chilled feelings, two spells of propulsion vomiting. He had been unable to read and had seen double vision on the T.V. His taste for coffee changed – he could not drink it and he was a heavy coffee drinker. He had frequent dizzy spells but we thought they were from being tired from the terrific headaches. He smell seemed normal, but his hearing seemed to be much keener and he heard the smallest noises and tried to listen to all conversations both near and further away. His gait was slower and he stumbled a lot. This dated back for several months. He would brush against things, always going to his right.

All Tuesday night Drs. studied his case history I had given him and observed him as they did. Drs. said he was very sick.

Wednesday, January 8

At 7 a.m. P.C. was carried to the X-ray room where pictures and tests were made by the specialists. Everything on the second floor of John Sealy was stopped except for P.C. I stayed with him through all the X-rays and reassured him. He asked no questions, only his eyes ask the question, "Why?"

About 10 a.m. the brain specialists told me they were going to do the arteriogram and there would not be room for me in this room. He asked me to wait in a nearby waiting room.

Two of my sisters were with me and we waited one-and-one-half hours. The brain surgeon finally came to us. We had seen P.C. on the stretcher pass the door. The surgeon said they had located the trouble and that it was a brain tumor. They had decided that from all they could tell by his history that it was a benign tumor near the surface on the left front of his brain (in his favor) and with an operation he would be alright in a few days.

The only thing that was unfavorable was the fact that it wasn't of such long duration. The longer it had been there, the better chance for recovery. [In other words, it would be a slow-growing tumor if it had been there a while. Later, the Drs. told Vera that the tumor had been malignant only for 1.5 months.]

We were told the surgery was not terribly

dangerous. So much depends on the type of tumor, and there are many types. In the case of P.C. it was near the surface on the left frontal lobe. We were told it was a benign tumor encapsulated and they would be able to lift it out in one piece. He was given nine out of ten chances to be alright after the operation.

How could this tumor have existed in his head and us not know it? How did he work through the Christmas rush at the [drug] store and even two days after Christmas with such a vicious thing gnawing away at his brain? Why did he not tell us how he felt?

Since P.C. was partially under anesthetics from the arteriogram the neuro-surgical staff thought it advisable to perform the operation without any delay. It seemed the only thing to do. In fact, there was no decision to make – it was already made by the surgeons. The surgeon told me to go home, and be back at the hospital by 6:30 p.m., that the operation was long and tedious and would take at least four hours and possibly much longer.

The operation took six or seven hours. He went into surgery at 11:30 a.m. and the operation was over at 6:30 p.m. We were not allowed to see him until 8 a.m. the following morning. He was kept in the recovery room overnight and given two pints of blood and we never knew what else.

The brain surgeon checked him at 7:30 and again at 9:30 after the operation. In fact, he told us around 9 p.m. that he was tired, that he was going home and have lunch, then a bath, rest a while and then he would have dinner. He had not eaten since breakfast. Brain operations are long and tedious.

The Hardest News for a Wife to Hear

At about 7:30 p.m., the surgeon came to us in the waiting room and told us the operation was over and P.C. was asleep and doing o.k. Those nine out of ten chances to be alright had been denied P.C., however.

The Dr. said the tumor was malignant and that he only had from four months to a year to live. P.C. would not have lived through the night without the operation. The pressure was so great and since the brain is within the hard shell of the skull with no room for expansion, the entire brain would have been destroyed. [Part of P.C.'s skull was removed so that the tumor could grow to the outside, thus there would be no pressure on the brain, and no pain.]

The incision was above the left ear in the form of a

horse shoe. His head was completely shaved. The Dr. explained he put the piece of skull to be removed back but did not tie it down thus it would bulge. (Sometimes as large as a grapefruit.) We questioned the Drs. at length, but because we knew so little about the disease, we were unable to understand all they told us. The bulge would give room for the tumor to grow and thus prolong life.

The Dr. added that they could not remove all of the tumor, but he removed as much as possible for him to be as normal as he could be. Suction was used to remove the one-half cup of the tumor that the Dr. removed. The tumor was of an infiltering, spidery type that creeps and burrows along the minute crevasses of the brain. This type slowly but surely destroys functions and is very difficult to remove. The neurosurgeon described it to us as a seaweed-like, spongy growth.

To have removed more of the tumor would have left P.C. blind and unable to move. Because the tumor was located near the speech area of the brain, the Dr. was sure P.C.'s speech would be impaired.

I was assured there would be no pain, that P.C. would be up and about although probably not well enough to do his usual work. The Dr. said that he would have setbacks at intervals and after each setback, he would never regain what he lost in the setback. The setbacks would become more frequent as time went on and finally he would be unable to get up and would get sleepier and sleepier. The end would not come unaware, so not to be afraid because we would know when the end was near. He said we would wake up one morning and he would have slipped away.

    X-ray treatments that are usually given to arrest the tumor was denied P.C. because they always make the patient worse before helping them. He was too sick for a spinal tap. P.C.'s condition was such that he was not able to take them. He couldn't afford to be any worse than he was already.

    Under no circumstances was P.C. to know how serious his condition was because he would not respond to anything if he did. He would lose his will to live. We were to treat him as though everything was a normal convalescence. Where the tumor was located would affect his speech. Speech would be impaired, but his intake of knowledge would be the same as ever. His mind would be as a telephone exchange – able to get the signals, but unable to convey them to others. Many things would go through his mind but in somewhat of a jumble.

    We were to give him all the love and security possible. In fact, live a normal life as far as possible. Because it was difficult to do, we did not think it impossible. We had to be like the cliff against which the waves continually break – to stand form and tame the fury of the water around it.

We took pleasure and comfort in one thing – in going from one act of love to another for our loved one. Thinking of God, thanking him for his blessings and begging for his help and mercy. Death, like birth is a mystery of nature and everything lasts only for a day.

If you were told you would die tomorrow or the next day after, you would not care much which one it was. The difference is too small to consider. So, we live from day to day, not knowing what tomorrow will bring, but it was always different. It was a succession of days and nights rather than days, weeks, or months.

We had to believe he would get well even though we knew he could not except for a miracle. But miracles do happen and each time he showed any improvement to me, this was the miracle about to happen. Even at the end, he breathed a few extra times and my hope soared to its brightest point – this was surely the miracle I had believed in all the time – then came the blackest of despair.

The Dr. warned us it would be increasingly difficult for P.C. to swallow but to feed him anything we wanted to except for alcoholic beverages. When he could no longer eat, the brain surgeon asked for his own sake not to let him starve as most brain tumor patients do. He asked us to take him to the hospital where he could be fed with a tube inserted into his stomach and this we did.

They never told us what caused a malignant tumor except that no one knows. It is as mysterious as life itself.

From the beginning, I was terrified with fear; numb with shock – absolutely unable to feel or speak.

Thursday, January 9

P.C. was carried to his room about 8 a.m. His head was bandaged with a huge turban bandage and his hands wrapped in gauze so that they looked like boxing gloves. This, we learned, was to keep him from tearing the bandage off his head. The Dr. said as soon as he knew why his hands were bandaged, we could remove the gauze. (It was only a couple of days.) His face was swollen and his eyes almost closed and with very dark circles under them, particularly the left eye.

The special nurses did everything they could to make him comfortable. One shaved him; every day except the day of the operation, my sister or myself shave him.

P.C. responded to everything that we told him to do – was cooperative in every way – except he would have nothing to do with any of the other patients in the ward. He seemed to resent them. They would pass and speak but he remained silent and unresponsive.

Since dehydration would tend to decrease the pressure inside his head, he could only have six cups of fluid a day, including water, milk, Cokes, soup and all liquids. We gave him three cups of milk a day, two Cokes and one cup of water.

Friday, January 10

The next morning seemed about as before the operation – he knew everything, responded, but now he did not talk as much as he had in the first ten days of his illness. The only speech he had was spontaneous. If you asked him a question, he could not answer.

I stayed with him every night. Sat and slept in a chair by his bed during his stay in the hospital. He never offered to ring for a nurse, but called me, or I would know what he wanted done without him saying anything.

He didn't care too much for the hospital food and

did not want to be raised much to eat. He seemed to enjoy his room full of flowers, sent by friends. I kept telling him everything was going to be alright during his illness. I told him that hundreds of times.

Sunday, January 12

On the third day after the operation, P.C. sat up in a chair for the nurses to make his bed. The bandages were removed from his hands.

P.C. had 17 visitors – his family, my family, our oldest daughter, and our pastor. He didn't seem to pay much attention except he cried as they came to see him.

I helped the Dr. dress his head and to me it was a horrible sight to see. This thing just couldn't happen.

Monday, January 13

On these successive days, P.C. sat up three or four times a day and with our help, walked to the bathroom. We walked him up and down the hall – walking to the end of the hall for an excellent view of the Gulf, or down to the elevator to sit in the lounge and watch the people. He tired very easily and was always anxious to get back to his bed.

The lights in the ward bothered him and many times he was restless until all lights were out, then he would sleep peacefully. Before bedtime he nurses brought him iced juice and around midnight he had a cup of milk. He was always hungry at breakfast and ate a good meal. The other meals, he was not so hungry, but ate fairly well at our insistence. Sometimes he had ice cream in the afternoon.

He was never any trouble. He would touch me with his hand. I was never out of reach of his hand at night. He squeezed my hand to let me know what he wanted. I would ask him if it was water, milk, or several other things and he always let me know what he wanted.

P.C. never seemed to understand the necessity for his head being elevated and he was always indicating for me to lower him. Of course we knew his head had to be elevated to relieve the pressure.

The entire neuro-surgical staff tried to work to find a way to help his necessary speech. They would question him at different times of day and night. Once they awakened him out of a deep sleep and asked him his age, where he lived, where he worked. His answer to all was "I don't know." Then when Dr. left, he smiled and said, "That didn't help me any did it?" We joked about it with him and told him we couldn't have answered the questions ourselves.

Tuesday, January 14

One night he took his Masonic ring off and put it under him. When I asked him about it, he showed me where it was.

We got steaks, fish, and the best food at Fetitoes [local restaurant] for him, but he never ate very much except for breakfast and he would eat all of it except coffee. Before he got sick he drank coffee all day. His tastes changed and he did not like it anymore.

Friday, January 17

It takes some time for the pathological report and we never learned this because on the ninth day after the operation P.C. had a setback and the report was unnecessary as far as we were concerned. The tumor had not changed, but the Dr.'s worst fears were confirmed. It was the fasted growing type – glioblastoma multiform.

When I raised his bed to feed him, he became real sick at his stomach and couldn't eat. He was very sleepy all day and we could tell a change had come over him.

Late in the afternoon he was carried to the dressing room with the neuro staff for his head to be dressed. It was then the surgeon learned that the operation was beginning to bulge and that the tumor was fast growing and the prognosis would be different. Now he was given only three or so months to live and we were told that the bulge might get as large as a grapefruit. The Dr. described his condition as "poorly." Now we were told he would never get up, but that he would have no pain and just get sleepier and sleepier to the end.

Wednesday, January 22

I assured P.C. daily that he was recovering from the operation on his head and I told him of plans when he went home. Now Jean, our daughter from Tacoma was coming. The Drs. refused to let her come to John Sealy.

They said it would only complicate the situation.

After P.C.'s lunch and nap I got ice cream for him and today he asked me about the hospital bill. I told him I had taken care of everything. He asked me, "What bank?", so I told him how all the arrangements had been made. He seemed satisfied and never mentioned it again.

Thursday, January 23

One day just before we came home, P.C. asked the Dr. as he was passing his bed, "How are things going?" The Dr. replied as he continued to walk, "Not so good. I'd be telling a lie of I said anything else."

The thoughts of what was ahead – each day was more horrible, more dreadful, and perhaps the reason we did not ask more questions was because we dared not because of what we might be told. He had gotten to where he would only sit up for a short time while his bed was made. Up to this time, he would sit in a chair by the bed several times a day. This day we borrowed a wheelchair from another patient and rolled him to the elevator and took him to the waiting room on the first floor. There was a drug store adjoining the waiting room and I bought him Cokes and gum. He drank and chewed gum as we told him to – but he didn't seem to be interested in anything or anyone. In fact, he didn't even seem to see them. The Drs. thought by bringing him home he might have a spontaneous reaction and respond to people and things. He would lie and stare into space with a faraway look in his eyes, never seeming to care about anything.

Saturday, January 25

P.C. was discharged and we came by ambulance from John Sealy to San Augustine. Left Galveston at 9 a.m. The trip of 200 miles took a frightful lot out of him. It was days before he seemed as well as when he left the hospital.

P.C. was excited about going home. I had been telling him for days we were coming home and on this morning as I started to bathe him before his breakfast, I told him this was the day we were going home and he said, "Let's go now!"

The Drs. removed the bandage and put a little green skull cap on him like the Drs. wear in surgery and that was the 2nd time we had seen where he was operated on. By this time the bulge was as large as half an egg cut lengthwise.

The ambulance had a blowout and P.C. understood and waited patiently for them to fix it. We arrived home at 1:30 and many of our friends were at the house. Our daughter, Melba, with friends, had prepared the house and gave us such a good welcome. P.C.'s room was banked with beautiful flowers – food cooked in the kitchen – everything we would need for several days. P.C. was so happy to be home on his own bed.

Sunday, January 26

Thirty-three friends came to see him. He cried when each one came.

There were difficult and unhappy days. Each day was different. We lived through the night to see what the next day would bring. We were never sure about anything, not only from day to day, but from moment to moment.

The first thing I did when we got home after the operation, I began to look up everything I could find on brain tumors. P.C. was to rest. He would not be able to read or look at T.V. Sit up as much as possible, walk to bathroom as long as possible. We even planned to carry him for a drive and show him his colored rent property.

P.C.'s room was perfect for his illness, large roomy, plenty of chairs for the family and friends to sit with him.

Friday, January 31

Knew what was going on. Whether or not P.C. knew it was cancer, we will never know. The chaplain who was so very sweet to us told us most brain tumor patients realized their condition and that after they got home from the hospital they had periods in which they would talk. P.C. tried on several occasions to talk to close friends, but could never make them understand what he wanted to say. He seemed to try to keep the family from knowing how sick he thought he was.

Saturday, February 1

He always held his toast or bread in his left hand when I fed him and ate it himself. He did this until we carried him to the hospital. Some days he could manage it better than others.

Sunday, February 2

We teased him about his "Yul Brenner" haircut and he would just smile. He enjoyed our jokes and seemed to enter into the spirit of them.

He wanted attention but I don't believe he would have complained if he had not gotten it. He would do anything I told him to do – even though sometimes it would take time. I swallowed for him thousands of times because it would take him so long.

Monday, February 3

Bob [son-in-law] left for Tacoma and when he told P.C. goodbye, he told him he had to go home and for him to hurry and get well. P.C. told him to have my sister come because we were going to need her.

Wednesday, February 5

My sister came and P.C. seemed so pleased. I was feeding him his lunch. When she went to eat her lunch, P.C. smiled and said to me, "You know it's funny, but I was just going to call her. Now don't tell her, but she had told me if you didn't treat me good to let her know and I didn't want to eat what you gave me." He almost laughed. I guess the nearest he came to a laugh during his illness.

Thursday, February 6

Men friends came at night and sat with P.C. Some days it would seem the day was endless and would never end. We would look up and there would be one f his friends to help us make the last hours of the day – offering help and encouragement.

Friday, February 7

He wanted everything as usual and his bedtime was 9:30. We would prepare for bed as usual. He wanted everyone to go to ed and would not go to sleep is anyone stayed up. so, we all went to bed – him to sleep and me to lie on the bed by him so he could touch me with his left hand.

Thursday, February 20

P.C. carried to hospital in an ambulance for a mult I & D [Incision and drainage of abscess]. We thought by the looks of the bulge of operation there was an infection, but three incisions were made, and no pus came out. The bandage was back on his head for a couple of days. The bulge was very large and extended to the front and back of the operations proper. Very red and bloodshot and soft.

The Drs. were not sure at first if the setback was caused by multiple eruption of small blood vessels or whether the growth of the tumor was the cause, or pressure from liquids.

The whole sixty-two days after the operation is a spotted memory – it seemed we were meeting one crisis after another. Our emotions were terrors and horrible.

Sunday, February 23

P.C. apparently picked things out of the air. All day he reached for things that were not there. He had a wild look out of his eyes, but through it all I could see glimmers of recognition. Most people that saw him thought he had lost the five senses, that he could neither see, hear, taste, smell, or feel. But they were wrong. The Dr. said he was still normal.

We discovered an infected hair follicle on the little finger of his right hand. We soaked it three times a day in salt water for two weeks before it was gone. He was real sensitive to the hot water, but was patient and showed signs of pain when we mashed the infection after soaking.

Monday, February 24

P.C. was better today – his eyes were back to normal and when I asked him if he could see he squeezed my hand.

He kept up the boldest kind of front, probably thinking he was keeping how serious he knew he was from us. I kept asking myself how could a woman go through this without children helping her. The brave and understanding spirit of our daughters, Melba and Jean, and the fact that we could all talk to him as casually as if death was not in the near future caused P.C. to respond and I'm sure relieved him of many fears.

His physical condition improved – he gained some weight. The heartbreaking thing was that the tumor was causing him to fade fast in spite of his better physical condition.

Wednesday, February 26

His birthday was a red letter day. We had his birthday party because the cake and ice cream was brought today and because he was feeling better than usual. Since each day was different, I was afraid to wait until the next day. He ate the ice cream and cake and knew it was his birthday party. We opened his packages and he seemed to enjoy them. His eyes followed me all the time.

Thursday, February 27

His birthday. We had another party – this time he ate the ice cream but was unable to eat the cake. He chewed gum a great deal for a few minutes each time.

Friday, February 28

We kept his fingernails manicured and this he really enjoyed. He was given penicillin for seven days and improved a lot – could swallow better.

Saturday, March 1

A friend sent some of her husband's birthday dinner – chicken and dressing, fruit salad, and a cake.

He coughed when he ate. Could have been from tiredness, but the Drs. warned us his throat would get very bad and be difficult to swallow. Liquids made him cough more than solids. The Drs. said he would have difficulty chewing.

He gradually got tireder and dozed and half dozed a great deal of the time.

The brain makes a human being what he is, memory, desire, impulse, even consciousness, sight, hearing, muscular movement, voice, and even the ability to chew. All this was what was being destroyed by an evil growth; the human mind in a chaotic struggle.

Sunday, March 2

Commode stopped up. [I love this entry, because it shows how life goes on, even in the midst of suffering. Often just doing the next thing that needs to be done, even if you can only do it mechanically, can be the greatest help to a grieving person.]

Monday, March 3

He was unable now to sit up for the bed to be changed and go to the bathroom, but we were able to anticipate his needs and things worked out well.

As the bulge grew larger P.C. would put his left hand on it. He was unable to speak much of the time, but the word was plain to see in his eyes – "Why can't I get well again? Why? Why?" – asked over and over, but still unanswered.

How could I explain to him? I asked myself, "Why should P.C. have to have this brain tumor? Why couldn't it have been something else so he could have a fighting chance? Where is the justice of it all? Was it accidental or just what did cause it? Why this struggle between life and death?"

The bulge continued to grow until it was as thick as a lemon and about twice as long – moving front to back. There was never any drainage, even though it looked as if it would burst. He had no dressing on his head – the operation was healed perfectly.

Once the Dr. tried to try to drain the bulge and thereby give P.C. some relief, but there was no drainage. Always the Dr. tested his grip, examined all his reflexes, tested his eyes and asked him questions. The bottom of is feet always brought a half smile. [Did the Dr. ask about them or check them each time he came?]

Usually in tumors of this type, the patient loses all functions, but P.C. did not do that. He was normal to the end. He waited patiently for the end. He had the best and most expert medical care the world of science knows.

Thursday, March 6

We geared our life to P.C.'s world. Sometimes the strain was almost unendurable. We had to keep up his will to live. It was as though the cord of life was wearing thin and we must do everything in our power to encourage him and give him hope if that was possible.

As I lay by him at night, he would put his left hand on me, I guess to be sure he was not alone. This night he kept feeling my rings and finally I asked him if he wanted his rings and he squeezed my hand. I put his rings (wedding ring and Masonic ring with diamond) on him and he seemed so pleased. At intervals he could move his right hand and foot.

I would shampoo his head each day and put baby oil on his scar.

P.C. could not walk or talk, lost his memory and was partially paralyzed on his right side. Still, it could have been worse. he could have become totally blind, unable to move or had some twitch constantly.

Friday, March 7

P.C. developed a lung infection. Was given penicillin – seemed to help. Each Friday during his illness seemed to be a crisis. Saturday the Dr. told us if he were not better by Monday we would take him to the hospital for some medicine he was unable to give at home. He had told us previously that he would tell us about three days before we would have to hospitalize him for the final term of his illness. We knew this was what he meant, but to keep P.C. from worrying and to make it seem routine, the Dr. used this method.

Sunday, March 9

He was very drowsy all today. He seemed quieter and sadder – breathing harder. It did not seem an emergency. He had been taking naps all during his illness.

All his sweetness and goodness seemed to be more evident. He was affectionate and wanted me to hold his hand. The afternoon, which could have been endless, passed with the speed of lightning.

Late in the afternoon he was as alert as when well. Talked to neighbors and told them goodbye with a smile and wave of the hand. He hugged the girls when they came to him for reassurance after Bobby [grandson] had crushed some glass in his mouth.

At dark he began to get worse, groaning with each breath, pulse very fast and respiration jumpy. We were up all night – gave him rest medicine for first time, two aspirin and rest medicine again. He indicated it was his throat hurting.

Monday, March 10

Carried to San Augustine Hospital. He seemed to be some better, but very difficult to swallow. Strangled more on liquids than solids. The look of bewilderment and questioning gave way to a look of resignation and submission. Dr. explained to him he would go to the hospital for a few days to take a new drug. He seemed to understand and went as an obedient child.

Tuesday, March 11

Several times during his meals I had to awaken

him, also when I shaved him I had to awaken him. At first when P.C. went to the hospital, Bobby and Kathy [grandchildren] would go in his room, look at the bed and go to another room, realizing it would seem, that this room was no longer a place to play and drink part of Granddaddy's Cokes and talk to him – sadly, it was not a place for the family to gather anymore.

Thursday, March 13

Not able to take liquids – ate solids though. An amusing even happened when my sister came while he was getting his bath and said to him, "I never saw the such, four women bathing one man!" He smiled and seemed to enjoy the fussing over him. He was modest to the end and would keep the sheet on him at all times.

Friday, March 14

Dr. said he only had a couple more days to live. He ate a couple bites of oatmeal but strangled so bad I was afraid to give him any more. Intravenous glycose infusions were started. He never ate again. He was unable to swallow the stomach tube. He would cough and it would come out of his mouth.

Finally I <u>knew</u>. It was his not being able to eat that gave me the utter finality. The feeling of impending tragedy and separation painful to contemplate because we had been together constantly. He looked tired and under a strain.

Saturday, March 15

Very bad all day. We had lots of company. He didn't seem to be disturbed by the company, but would raise his left hand and move his legs, helped us to turn him. He still responded when he answered our questions by squeezing our hand. The glucose infusions were continued to the end.

Sunday, March 16

Responded to amusing incidences told him. He seemed better and the Dr. thought he would survive perhaps another week. In the a.m. he had his bath as usual and I shaved him. Felt his face when I shaved him. He seemed to enjoy his shave. But about noon he went to sleep and slept most of the p.m. Late in the afternoon he had to have his throat cleared twice with the suction machine. His tongue was thick and coated. We used grease to keep it moist.

Monday, March 17

P.C. passed away at 7:15 a.m. at the hospital. Our daughter [I don't know whether it was Melba or Jean.] spoke at the door and he turned his eyes to see her and squeezed her hand. He had difficulty breathing all night and around 4:30 a.m. the nurses used the suction machine to clear his throat, but by 5:30 it was apparent the end was near.

It seemed he patiently, in tranquility, waited for the end. Not but one sigh – an eternity of long breaths and as I held his hand and repeated the 23rd Psalm, he slipped away. When I released his hand, it was as though I placed it into the nail-scarred hand of Jesus.

Tuesday, March 18

Funeral 2 p.m.

Buried at Liberty Hill Cemetery 2:30 p.m.

It seemed I could feel no grief, only a job accomplished, one that must be done. With each beat of my heart, it was saying, "Death."

Everything seemed unreal. I was neither hot nor cold, hungry nor thirsty. Darkness and daylight were the same. I shivered as with a chill, but I had to control myself – this had to be. My marriage was over with P.C. but my life wasn't. Somehow I must take heart and take hold.

A constant procession of visitors – gifts and flowers poured in. They brought cakes, pies, fruit, canned goods, baked hens, etc., etc. as evidence of the sorrow of our friends and their helpfulness.

Tuesday evening: The house is cold, not really from lack of heat, and empty – that paralyzed me with fear. The grief that I had been choking back engulfed me. This was <u>real</u>.

[The darkness of nighttime is often the most difficult time for a person who is grieving. During the day, one can be distracted with other things, but at night the reality of one's situation comes crashing down. If you are grieving, let Vera's words from the day of her husband's funeral comfort you:]

The sweet majesty of the words of the 23rd Psalm that had sustained me for the last eighty days reached in and calmed me and gave me strength. I knew somehow that God would see me through this day.

The Days Following

[These are some scattered notes my grandmother wrote and I have compiled them here in one section. These notes show how a grieving person moves from disquiet to peace, and back again. This is normal during the grieving period. After a while, with faith, the peaceful moments become more frequent than the disquieted ones.]

In our home – these four walls – there had been so much love and work and faith and hope. We went ahead with prayers in our hearts because we knew it was a crucial time.

"Why?" I ask it desperately, confusedly, almost every hour of the day. "Why did the one I love have to die so young?" Fifty-five is young now. Life is like a golden thread – so easily snapped.

The icy fear that gripped my heart – puzzled grief that knows no words. Heaviness of despair – it came as a complete shock, unexpected, bewildering.

Those terrible nights – one can never forget them. I am thankful that we were cared for through all of them. When we do everything that we can, then we can ask God to do the rest.

In the days and nights of sorrow and trouble, God's presence and sympathy grow very sure.

P.C. is still alive. He lives in our hearts – his influence and personality are still felt and remembered by many: the treasured moments we have known – the glad "Good Morning!" and the wonderful "Good Night."

I can take pleasure and comfort in one thing: in going from one act of love to another, thinking of God. When circumstances disturb you, return to yourself quickly – because it is difficult to do, do not think it is impossible.

[Two scriptures, besides the 23rd Psalm, gave Vera particular comfort:]

"And we know that all things work together for good to them that love God, to them who are the called according to his purpose." Romans 8:28

"But those who hope in the Lord will renew their strength. They will soar on wings like eagles; they will run and not grow weary, they will walk and not be faint." Isaiah 40:31

God gives power for every crisis. Power to run if one must run; to come through as a conqueror; to walk and not faint. Few soar, many run, all walk.

[One statement of Vera's in this book that really speaks to me is this one:]

We took pleasure and comfort in one thing – in going from one act of love to another for our loved one. Thinking of God, thanking him for his blessings and begging for his help and mercy.

[Written by Shelby in January 2020: My own husband is ill at this time, but he is responding well to treatment. Vera knew what my days are now like: I too move from one act of love or kindness or compassion to another, and need help and encouragement to do so. I have seen blessing after blessing given as little gifts to us during this time of illness, and I look forward each day to see what new blessings are in store.]

[*At that time, my husband anticipated surgery that we thought would be the cure for his cancer. However, it was not to be. Only three months after I wrote this, my husband would join my grandfather.*]

What the 23rd Psalm Meant to Me
by Vera Nooner

"The Lord is my Shepherd"

Someone to look after me and care for me. What can happen to one who has the Lord for his Shepherd? How wonderful to have a Lord, to believe in God. A shepherd knows his sheep. Not even a sparrow falls that the Lord is not mindful of it. Why should I worry, no matter what happens, if the Lord is my Shepherd?

P.C. knew the Lord as his Shepherd. The Lord would take care of him even in this illness and even in death.

"I shall not want"

No matter what befalls me, God will take care of my needs. I shall not want for spiritual strength. I shall not want physically because god will guide me to do what will be best for me. Even though I will be alone, God will see that what I do not have will be what I do not want.

What P.C. needs God will supply. He will give him strength, calmness, and patience. All the things that would be best for him, he will have.

"He maketh me to lie down in green pastures"

Rest and comfort will come. "To lie down" – that's rest. "Green pastures" – that's comfort and ease. To me in my sorrow, rest and peace would one day come, even though it comes late.

That was what God gave P.C. from day to day. To me, it describes his death – rest and peace in beautiful surroundings.

"He leadeth me beside the still waters"

God was leading me to places of renewed courage, strength and faith. If the Lord leads, why should we be afraid to follow? He doesn't ask us to go where he has not already gone.

The "still waters" are the deep and abiding faith and knowledge of God: the things that really count and that give depth to our life. In stillness is where you are face to face with God.

God was leading P.C. in all his illness and to be an obedient follower, he had to go all the way. The way was beside the still waters – the knowledge of God and his goodness.

"He restoreth my soul"

No matter how troubled and terrified I became, God would restore my soul and make me understand that he was God and that all would be well, even though I could not understand, and when the "whys" came into my mind, he restored my faith.

God would take P.C.'s soul when the end came and would keep him forever.

"He leadeth me in the paths of righteousness for his name's sake"

As long as he leads and I would follow, I would not take the wrong path for his name's sake.

God would be with P.C. and lead him right through this life into the next for his name's sake.

"Yea, though I walk through the valley of the shadow of death, I will fear no evil, for thou art with me"

As I go through this death, there will be no fear that the Lord is not present to help and comfort both P.C. and me.

God would be with him when I could go no farther. My limitation was God's opportunity. He could give help that no one else could.

In death, P.C. would be calm and serene and all his fears would be erased. Tranquility would be his last earthly sensation. God would guide him to his heavenly home.

"Thy rod and thy staff, they comfort me"

God's rod provides correction and his staff a guide.

[We know we live safely inside the bounds of God's rules for living the best life possible and know that he guides us all the way. Naturally, this is comforting.]

[God would safely guide P.C. through his illness and home to forever be with his Lord.]

"Thou preparest a table before me in the presence of mine enemies"

God had prepared a table for P.C. with everything good, beautiful, fine, and lovely he had ever wanted and was leading him to this table by way of death. All the evil forces that had disturbed him and kept him from doing the good he would have were pushed aside as P.C., led by God, approached the table. To me it proved he had overcome evil.

"Thou anointest my head with oil"

God was giving P.C. all the calmness and healing and gentleness and understanding he needed to face death.

"My cup runneth over"

If I could only remember that no matter what happened, that because P.C. had God as his Lord and Shepherd, that was all that really mattered. That was the cup running over. More blessings and love than his cup could hold.

"Surely goodness and mercy shall follow me all the days of my life"

Because P.C. believed in God and was led by him, surely – as sure as there is a God – all the goodness and mercy that God could give to him would be his. Day by day, his goodness and mercy would be given to P.C. as he needed it.

"And I shall dwell in the house of the Lord forever."

P.C. would be living with God for eternity – in God's house, sharing all the things that God offers to his guests and shares with them. A guest in God's house [is a wonderful thing to be, with pleasures and joy at God's right hand forever.]

PART II:

Granddaughter Shelby Boyett's Story

Bryan and Shelby walking down the aisle after taking their wedding vows, 2 April 1977

Bryan and Shelby in the early years

Bryan unpacking after one of the couples' many moves, 1997

Twenty-fifth wedding anniversary, 2002

Bryan and Shelby on a cruise, 2000

Dementia actually changes brain function, structure, and ability. You will rarely win an argument [with] dementia.

Very Well Health.com

Dementia takes away our ability to analyze, label, and interpret. We lose the ability to drift away on memories or to anticipate or plan for the future.

Judy Cornish

Our Life Together

My husband, Bryan, and I had a long marriage of forty-three years. I met him on 4 October 1974, only a week and a half after I turned eighteen, so I knew him my whole adult life. His opinions shaped mine, and vice-versa. I depended on him for so much, and I like to think he depended on me for things too.

We met my senior year in high school in a small town in East Texas. (Bryan was a sophomore in college.) I attended a party after a football game with four other girlfriends and this guy I didn't know kept putting an 8-track tape in the machine with music that I liked. Others kept taking it out. I got someone to introduce us. Bryan ended up taking me home that night and we talked for an hour and a half in my parents' driveway. Only two months later, he proposed. We were sitting out by a lake and I didn't understand what he said at first and he had to repeat the proposal! At least he didn't give up!

We didn't get married for two more years, as I knew

my parents would not approve of my marrying right out of high school. We spent a great deal of time together, however. I remember my mother saying that I wouldn't see so much of Bryan if we were married than I was seeing of him back then.

We married on 2 April 1977, while I was on spring break in my second year at Tyler Junior College. (My parents didn't have enough money to send me to a more expensive school at that time.) I completed the last month of my Associate in Applied Science degree and Bryan stopped attending school for a while and supported us and then we finished our Bachelor's degrees together, graduating at the University of Texas with me walking just behind him across the stage to receive our diplomas.

After a very brief honeymoon spent in Dallas and mostly taken up by car problems, we started out our married life in Tyler, Texas and spent our weekends exploring the area. We also went to Dallas often to shop and visit museums. I remember seeing all the large archaeological exhibits that came to Dallas or Fort Worth, including Ramses II. One of our favorite pursuits was to visit used bookstores looking for reading treasures.

We never spent too much money on vacations, but managed to find good deals and enjoyed visiting the Caribbean and the east coast beaches in the U.S. When I sold cruises for a couple of years, we took six cruises in that time and spend many hours in Miami touring the cruise ships on which we hadn't sailed.

During our marriage, we moved sixteen times – sometimes just across town, other times, halfway across the country – and lived in four states: my native Texas, Georgia, Florida, and North Carolina. Of course, it was more complicated than that, with a move to Georgia, then back to Texas, then back to Georgia, then to North Carolina, then to Florida, then back to North Carolina!

We had a great time in Georgia, both in exploring the Cherokee heritage of the area and with trips to the North Georgia Mountains on many weekends. Our New Year's Day tradition was to go to the Rich Mountain Wilderness and hike a little and then sit by a fast-running mountain stream, listening to the relaxing sound. It was always almost deserted there on New Year's Day and we enjoyed having the wilderness to ourselves.

Our time in Florida was brief by comparison, but we enjoyed the lovely Lantana Beach in Palm Beach County and befriended some bright green parrots who lived in the trees close to our apartment. I spent every day at the beach while he worked! Our house here in Charlotte didn't sell while we were in Florida, and so we moved back to Charlotte at the end of a year. That was our sixteenth move, but back to our fourteenth house.

My husband faced challenges and lay-offs in his career in contract hardware, and after our last move, he tried several different career paths in order to stay in one place, finally ending up in management in the self-storage industry when we got to Charlotte. Partly because of all these moves, I never developed a career beyond some years spent in early childhood education and a brief but enjoyable time as an adjunct instructor at a technical school in Atlanta, as well as owning my own cruise travel agency for a bit. Then I discovered writing – what I was meant to do all along.

Our lives were good for so many years: for at least twenty-five years, when we were in Acworth, north of Atlanta, and had a nice party for our anniversary that replicated the refreshments served at our wedding; for at least thirty years, when I remember on our anniversary that he was out of work and apologized to me, saying that he was sorry we couldn't do something big for that anniversary; and when he wrote a book dedication that named me as his "soulmate." That was 2007, and close around this time, he developed an underlying anger that I couldn't understand.

Fear, worry, depression, anger, and low self-esteem are common [in dementia patients]. The person may become dependent and cling to you. He or she may not remember your life together and feelings toward one another. **The person may even [become infatuated] with someone else.**

National Institute on Aging
U.S. Department of Health and Human Services

Our Dementia Journey

My husband's last illness would first appear to be straightforward: he developed bladder cancer, and it was already at Stage 3B when it was discovered in August of 2019. However, another vicious killer was already at work in his body – vascular dementia: a silent, stalking enemy that went unrecognized by the medical community. Bryan had developed symptoms that concurred with Frontotemporal Dementia, or FTD.

I want to make clear at this point that I was only told about Bryan's loss of gray matter – described as "generalized brain shrinkage" – five days before he died. So I lived with his hurtful behavior for several years without knowing why his personality had changed.

FTD can affect either the frontal or temporal lobes of the brain. Just as my grandfather lost function in the temporal lobe of his brain due to a tumor, and thus his speech was affected, my husband lost brain matter in the frontal lobe of his brain (and elsewhere in his brain) due to lack of oxygen and thus his behavior was affected.

70% of the cases of FTD occur in persons under age sixty-five, with onset in the early to mid-50s. This is why the disease often goes undetected: no one is thinking about dementia occurring in a person in his fifties or even early sixties and thus no testing is done to determine if this is the cause of the person's problems. With the person still being rather high functioning, this disease – especially the behavioral variant – preys on its victims unnoticed. One can make other excuses for the person's behavior and the idea of dementia is never addressed until the person's case is well advanced. So many families suffer abusive treatment from a family member without knowing why. I hope that hearing about Bryan's symptoms will help someone to recognize those same type of symptoms in their loved one, and encourage them to get their loved one whatever help is available instead of suffering in silence.

> The frontal lobe is the part of the brain that controls important cognitive skills in humans, such as emotional expression, problem solving, judgment, and sexual behaviors. It is, in essence, the "control panel" of our personality and our ability to communicate. (Healthline Medical Network.)

The disease of FTD itself is sometimes hereditary, sometimes not. The need for the development of reliable physiologic markers for the disease is a pressing one. "Current measures of severity and disability do not stage or track the progression of disability in Frontotemporal Dementia (FTD) well." ("Estimating Severity of Illness and Disability in Frontotemporal Dementia: Preliminary Analysis of the Dementia Disability Rating (DDR)," Chiadi U. Onyike, Kelly L. Sloane, Shawn F. Smyth, Brian S. Appleby, David M. Blass, and Peter V. Rabins.)

The clinical definition of FTD is as follows (Bold mine): "FTD is a clinically and pathologically heterogeneous familial and sporadic neurogenerative disorder usually manifesting, at its onset, as focal **disintegration of temperament, judgment, conduct**, and speech." (Chaiadi U. Onyike, MD, MHS and Janine Diehl-Schmid, MD, "The Epidemiology of Frontotemporal Dementia.") Eventually, FTD evolves into a "global dementia" (Kertesz, McMonagle, Blair, Davidson, and Munoz, "The Evolution and Pathology of Frontotemporal Dementia," *Brain: a Journal of Neurology*, 2005.)

The frontal lobe regulates a person's behavior. Thus, if one has the behavioral variant of the disease, accounting for 60% of cases, one experiences *major* changes in behavior. "This results in a behavioral phenotype beginning with **combinations of indifference, impatience, carelessness, jocularity, insensitivity, distractibility, impulsiveness, stereotyped behaviors, compulsions, and rigid routines**." (Bold mine.) Bryan exhibited all of these behaviors, some more often than others. "Non-typical presentations feature...parkinsonism or motor neuron disease." (Bradley Boeve, "Alzheimer Disease and Associated Disorders," 2007.) I mention this last non-typical presentation because I had noticed that Bryan had begun at times to have an involuntary shaking of his head over the last few years. At times this shaking was quite noticeable. Once I even asked him if he was deliberately shaking his head and he told me he was not.

Bryan displayed the symptoms of the behavioral variant of this type of dementia (even though his dementia was caused by lack of oxygen), which gradually caused him to **disregard social boundaries; to say and do inappropriate things; and to behave impulsively and carelessly, perhaps even criminally** – "A gross decline in conduct," according to Chiadi U. Onyike, MD, MHS and Janine Diehl-Schmid, MD.

Loss of brain matter in the frontal lobe causes a **loss of inhibition** and a **loss of impulse control**. This is why the diseased person can do things their conscience would normally prohibit them from doing. Dementia even explains why Bryan suddenly wanted to shop for clothes more often – when he had never been interested in clothes shopping before – and why he collected excessive amounts of numerous other items – some of them rather expensive.

Bryan also experienced deterioration in his reasoning and judgment, and he lost empathy and concern for others, chiefly members of his family. Here are some small examples of how his treatment of his family and his work relationships suffered:

1) **His wife** – he repeatedly spoke to me in a hateful voice and then did not remember doing so afterwards. (Once I actually said aloud to him that I wished he wouldn't speak to me in a certain tone of voice because, "It sounds like you hate me." He looked at me questioningly and blankly and replied, "I don't hate you.")

He also told others strange and untrue things about me, such as that I had "ridiculed him, belittled him, and manipulated him."

2) **His father** – Bryan began refusing to call or speak to his father.

3) **His siblings** – after a visit to his father's house,

where all his siblings were together for the first time in many years, Bryan came home with nothing but negative feedback about his brothers and his sister. He said that they had "ganged up on him" and he felt verbally attacked by them. They didn't understand what was important to him, such as reenacting in World War II garb, and they were "so stupid" because they didn't agree with his political ideas.

4) **His immediate supervisor** – Bryan accused his boss of "putting him down" and "insulting" him constantly.

None of these above comments could be taken at face value, because they came from the "dementia mind," not from the real Bryan himself.

As the dementia progresses to the middle stage, a person's behavioral disturbances become more frequent and consistent, and in Bryan's case, more daring and hurtful. By this time, his inhibitions were down and he could do things he would never dream of doing in his right mind.

During this time, he had only slight memory loss. (If he had more, he covered for it well.) This distinguishes FTD and vascular dementia from Alzheimer's disease, where the primary symptom is memory loss. He did misplace items such as keys quite often. It almost became a joke to me, because when he would "lose" something, he would look for it for a considerable amount of time, searching all over the house and even in our vehicles. After a while I would say, "Go back and look in the first place you looked." Every time, that is exactly where the item would be and the rest of his time had been wasted. Now, anyone can misplace their keys from time to time. However, this scenario happened with increasing frequency until it was more common than not, even though I tried to establish "collecting spaces" to help him keep up with his things.

In the last few months before his death, his mental condition worsened considerably, possibly a sign the disease was entering the last stage, which appears almost identical to late stage Alzheimer's disease. (Of course, chemotherapy and surgery also contributed greatly to Bryan's downward spiral.) From the deteriorated condition of his brain as shown on CT scans, taken in 2017 and 2020, which showed a brain age approximately twenty years older than his actual age, Bryan had been developing dementia perhaps as long as fifteen years. Because the disease progresses at different rates even in the same person at different times, it is impossible to tell for certain exactly when this disease began in my husband's brain, but I have been able to think back in time and discover things he said and ways in which he acted that only make sense in the light of dementia, allowing me to estimate when he began having problems.

Descriptions of the disease explain how sometimes one can have FTD and it not progress very much for ten years or so and then progress rapidly after that. That actually seems to fit what happened in Bryan's case. (This would be due to blockage getting progressively worse, in his case.) A person with FTD lives with the disease about seven years on average. The disease can range from a person dying very quickly, in about three years, to a maximum of seventeen years. Most deaths are caused by infection (which Bryan's was, but likely his was more directly the fault of chemotherapy treatments lowering his immune system).

My hope in telling this painful story of my husband's illness is that someone who witnesses uncharacteristic behavior in a loved one will have that love one undergo diagnostic tests to determine if the cause of this or her behavior could be dementia. It would have been so helpful if we could have known from the very beginning that Bryan's behavior had a medical explanation. Much pain, especially my own, could have been avoided. Bryan was too young for dementia, or so I thought, and so his turning into a completely different – and unlikable – person was inexplicable at first. I never thought to "have his head examined," although I may have flippantly suggested it at some point, as all wives do.

My husband was always a kind sort of person. Oh, he could be selfish just like anyone else. Early in our marriage, his response to me asking if he could dry the dishes while I washed – I was thinking of a time of bonding while doing a shared task – was to buy me a portable dishwasher! When he had his heart set on one of his hiking trips with a friend, nothing could dissuade him. But most of the time, he was thoughtful and cheerful – he didn't mind getting something down off a top self (he was 6'1") or unscrewing a tight jar lid or taking me some place I wanted to go. All that cheerfulness was to change, however.

When we moved to North Carolina in 2004, after a year in Florida, he gradually began to act differently. He often became agitated, irritable, and angry. Even while in Florida, I sensed that he was acting a little strangely. There he was in a new job, and he was more concerned about buying office furniture than about perfecting the job into what he wanted it to be. I even questioned him about it once, not wanting to pry, but his behavior seemed odd to me and I wondered what he was thinking. I didn't receive a satisfactory answer. Little did I know it, but my not receiving a good answer to an inquiry was to become a persistent problem – the norm rather than the exception.

When the Florida job fell through, we came to North Carolina and he built a 20' x 20' deck in our backyard all by himself. A few years later, I could not ask him to do anything around the house without him becoming angry. Even small jobs were too much trouble for him, and he made me feel so badly for asking that I soon learned not to ask. I couldn't understand why he no longer seemed to care about his own home: window sills were rotting and the outside needed paint and the siding needed to be replaced. I assumed it was money that was the problem, so I didn't press these issues.

I would never have thought that this lack of care for his home was a sign of my husband's dementia – but it is a "textbook" symptom. Then my husband began to make comments about how he didn't see how he could continue working for the rest of the years until retirement. He never gave an explanation, but just said that he didn't see how he could. He deliberately took an assistant manager position instead of a manager position at his work. His stated reason was that with his experience, he got paid almost as much as a manager, so why take on the extra responsibility?

I had no idea at the time, but a lack of motivation and apathy are both signs of dementia. He may have actually realized that he was not able to perform his job as well as he used to and was covering up for this by his comments. This "covering up" behavior is typical of those with dementia and Alzheimer's. The ill person feels the need to try to hide what is going wrong with them, for fear of what will happen to them if the extent of their problems should become known to others. The person also doesn't want to face the fact that anything is wrong with them, as none of us would.

The sad fact is, I assume Bryan didn't know what was happening to him. He was unable to understand why he felt restless and unsettled and unable to cope with life's situations. He acted the stoic male with me, however, and didn't share his concerns with me. There was a point in 2016 when he said something to me that was in a way a cry for help, but I didn't recognize it at the time. He said, "You have to let me do the things I want to, **so I can feel like myself again**." There he had given me a clue that something was going terribly wrong, but it was so subtle I didn't hear it. I was only worried about the behavior he wanted me to let him continue.

People with dementia are looking for

something comfortable and familiar over which they have some degree of control. (Mental Help.net)

Bryan also became what I was calling "hyper-sensitive" to supposed insults. He complained all the time about his various bosses. One especially was "always putting him down." I would ask why didn't he politely say something to the person about stopping the unwanted behavior, but Bryan always refused to do this, saying it would only make it worse. Thus, he had a situation that was constantly making him angry but he would do nothing to make the situation go away. Unfortunately, that type of situation became true at home and with his extended family as well.

Soon, Bryan would be angry at me and I would not know the reason why. Only occasionally could I find out a reason, and when I did, the reason was always untrue and exhibited a good bit of paranoia on his part. On one occasion, we were driving somewhere in the car and he became angry, saying, "There you go again!" I was frankly puzzled, as I had only just said that if I were in his particular circumstance, I was the type who wouldn't be able to wait, I would have to ask my boss for an answer to a question if it were troubling me. Bryan went on to explain that I was "telling him what to do all the time." One can see that his interpretation of events and facts was skewed in a negative way.

On another day, we sat on our deck in the sunshine and it was a day where nothing had gone wrong – no bad news or phone calls. He seemed angry at me, however. I decided to pressure him a little to try to find out why he exhibited underlying anger. His answer was surprising and venomously spoken, "How about that for forty years you have corrected me front of other people!" He seemed to think that I constantly interrupted him and corrected him in front of others, and that this meant that I thought I was better than he. This was shocking to hear, of course, simply because we are used to believing what our loved one says.

How does one apologize for doing something for forty years – something that you weren't even doing? It was difficult, but I found myself apologizing for things I hadn't done just to calm him down. I later found out I had done the right thing: it's better to appear to agree with a person with dementia and then gently redirect the person's thoughts in another direction. By the end of his life, and only through the grace of God, I could see that all these words truly came from the "dementia mind," not from my loving husband.

Judy Cornish, founder of the Dawn Method, had the

answer that I was looking for that day on the deck. She states that:

> Patients with dementia who are mean and aggressive are most likely feeling anger, fear, and embarrassment because they've been asked to use skills that they no longer have. It's those losses to the person's skills that set them up for embarrassment and feeling mistreated and lead them to react by being mean...We inadvertently embarrass people and unintentionally belittle or frustrate them without realizing what we've done by asking them to do something that they cannot do. We then find ourselves on the receiving end of a verbal blow with no idea what went wrong and their response seems unwarranted or crazy.

She goes on to add that, if your loved one is "overnight being 'difficult' about something, it's because that skill just became unavailable to them."

The losses one experiences with dementia are skills that a mentally healthy person cannot imagine ever losing. The four major losses are:

1. Rational Thinking Loss #1 – Becoming unable

to understand "why." Dementia takes away the person's ability to perceive relationships between facts, such as understanding "how," "why," "when," "who," and "what." If you try to explain why they need to do something, or what went wrong with something, or how to do something, the dementia patient will be unable to follow your train of thought and will end up embarrassed or maybe even conclude that you're making fun of them. This causes much of the anger displayed by dementia patients. I imagine that this was the cause of the arguments Bryan would try to pick with me when we were driving somewhere and at other times.

2. Rational Thinking Loss #2 – Becoming unable to see cause and effect. "When your loved one refuses to put on a coat before going out in the snow, they are not being difficult. You are asking them to do what is now impossible for them." (Cornish.)

I will never forget the day that I sat eating a snack with good friends while we looked out the window at the snow falling – and talked about why on earth Bryan had insisted on going camping alone on a weekend like this. None of us could understand his behavior. Loss #2 was the explanation for it.

A year or so later, Bryan gave me another example

of Loss #2 when he insisted on taking his motorcycle, loaded with camping gear, toward the mountains. Unfortunately, he wouldn't tell me exactly where he was going, or where he planned to spend the night. He didn't call that first night, so I had no idea if he was dead or alive. This was a really good example of the lack of empathy and the "selfishness" that comes with dementia. I had almost grown used to being treated this way by the time this took place, but others who knew us could not believe he could be so unfeeling. I didn't know why he was acting so unfeeling either, and it was breaking my heart.

This loss was also another reason why Bryan let our home deteriorate and why he stopped doing any repairs. He couldn't see that there would be a consequence of not doing the repair I asked him to do. And perhaps he had forgotten how to do the repair and so made a big show of not wanting to comply in order to cover up that fact.

3. Rational Thinking Loss #3 – Becoming unable to follow sequences. This loss could greatly impact trying to hold down a job. I am amazed that Bryan kept a job as long as he did. Following the facilities' guidelines for how to speak with customers, how to close a sale, or how to enter information in the computer must have all become progressively harder for him to do.

4. Rational Thinking Loss #4 – Becoming unable to prioritize. The patient with dementia becomes unable to understand why one thing is more important than another, such as why keeping doctor appointments are necessary or why there might ever be a need to hurry.

> The person with dementia feels confused, frustrated, and angry more and more often.
> Alzheimer's Research UK

Dementia Care Central states that the middle stages of dementia are when anger and aggression are most likely to start occurring as symptoms. Other worrying habits like wandering, hoarding, and compulsive behaviors begin at this time as well. If I could pinpoint the first time I sensed this underlying anger in Bryan, I could perhaps determine when he entered the middle stage, but it occurred so gradually that I have no idea when it began.

One day I did something that was perhaps not exactly kind, but I felt it was necessary. I pinned one of Bryan's friends down and got him to tell me what he actually thought of Bryan's behavior. I needed to know that it was not all in my imagination that he was treating me so unkindly. I wanted to know that someone else who knew Bryan fairly well could also see that his behavior was unkind. The friend was reluctant, of course, but finally responded that Bryan was selfish and opinionated. I had personally witnessed Bryan arguing an unimportant point with this friend one evening to the point of embarrassment.

The following quote was one I found most helpful:

> Sufferers may be more **irritable, selfish, inconsiderate, and obstinate.** They may behave in ways that are socially embarrassing. They may lose interest in hobbies and appear content to sit doing nothing. Alternatively, they may be restless.
>
> Can the sufferer alter his/her behaviour? Sometimes sufferers may seem to be behaving in a deliberately awkward or selfish way. However, they are not being deliberately awkward. **Their behaviour is the result of brain disease and is not under their control.** Their apparent selfishness is because the condition results in loss of mental flexibility: **sufferers are no longer able to put themselves in someone else's shoes and see things from another person's perspective.**
>
> Is the sufferer aware of his symptoms? In general sufferers are not aware of changes in

themselves. Even if they notice changes they typically do not show appropriate concern.

(*Cerebral Function Unit*, UK, bold mine.)

Bryan certainly exhibited these qualities. He was definitely irritable, selfish, inconsiderate, and obstinate. This article was very helpful to me because it states right out that "the sufferer is no long able to see things from another person's perspective." This explains why Bryan could at times seem not to care about my feelings any more than he cared about a piece of furniture in the same room. I am also comforted by the statement that his behavior was the result of brain disease and was not under his control. He didn't mean to be deliberately cruel to me – although it would have been lovely to have known this at the time!

In an article by James M. Ellison, MD, MPH of the Swank Center for Memory Care, entitled, "What Are the Stages of Frontotemporal Dementia?," FTD was described by the example of the compiled case of "Emily and Joseph." The article read, "When Emily was upset about a conflict at work, Joseph (age sixty-two) shrugged off her concern and didn't seem to care as he always had in the past." This was a real problem for me during Bryan's illness. He lost empathy for me a good deal of the time. I could cry in front of him and beg him to change his behavior, and he would not even respond. No sympathy or kind words were forthcoming from him. I never received a real apology or saw any remorse in him for the hurtful things he did. Only now can I remember the rather blank look on his face and realize it was there because he had lost the part of his brain that would have allowed him to understand my request and to have cared about it. He did not actually remember doing what I was telling him he had said or done, and he was hoping that if he just waited it out, I would give up and stop asking him about it; then he would not be forced to admit he didn't remember. At the time, I just wondered how he could be so cold and unresponsive.

> Showing no emotion – it's the first part of the brain to begin to deteriorate. [The dementia patient experiences a] lack of help from the frontal lobe to properly process their thoughts. (Hope Hospice.)

In another medical article, Ellison used the fictitious name of "Richard" to describe more problems that arise in a person with FTD: "Richard, age fifty-six, surprised his family when he splurged on a new Porche. His friends realized something was very wrong when he began to stay out late at night, frequenting bars, and flirting with young women." This type of behavior was the worst behavior of Bryan's with which I had to deal.

> You don't have your loved one to confide in and lean on…How ironic, the one person who would have been your "go to" for such things is now the one you need support and understanding dealing with. (Judy Cornish.)

This was the "beginning of sorrows" for me – a time that left me with no peace of mind. Only my faith in God kept me going during this awful time. I could no longer lean on my husband for support and strength, as he was the one who was hurting me, and so I turned to God to provide my lifeline, and of course, God was there for me.

By 2007, Bryan was speaking with a particular woman more often because he wrote a small book about the woman's son's enlistment in the Marine Corps. He had become friends with the young man. The boy's father had left the family and so Bryan "mentored" him, supposedly as a substitute father figure. Mentoring the young man and standing up for him in his desire to enter military service seemed like a positive thing. However, it brought him ever closer to the boy's mother (I will call her "Betsy"). After a few more years, their relationship began to take on an unhealthy tinge.

Bryan didn't tell me he was writing the book, so this was the beginning of him hiding things from me. He used the letters the young man wrote to him and the letters the young man wrote to his mother to compose the contents of the book. Bryan wrote the book during 2007 and published it in 2008. (Back then, one had to use a local vanity press to publish a book like this.) The young man found being written about in that manner rather embarrassing, but he had to take it in stride as it was a "done deal." In the dedication of this book, Bryan mentioned me and called me his "bride and soul mate." The phrase "soul mate" would be one I grew to dislike.

I am sure that at this juncture, the young man had no idea that his mentor and his mother were going to pursue an inappropriate relationship. That is what is *sneaky*, if you will, about dementia in the early days – it moves so slowly one doesn't recognize what is going so very wrong until it has already happened. In hindsight it is certainly much easier to see the big picture than it was at the time we were living through it.

In notes written at a later time, Bryan said that he: "Didn't feel confident to express myself [for] fear of criticism. It took encouragement to write to bring me out of seclusion and gain self-confidence." He felt that the changing of his personality from a shy, quiet person into a much more outgoing person who monopolized conversations and talked longer than others wanted to hear, was coming "out of seclusion," and was thus a good thing.

Normally, one would agree that being a little more outgoing could be a good thing for a shy person. However, Bryan was actually expressing dementia in this way in the days he spent in hospital after his surgery. He tried to entertain all the nurses who came to his room by telling jokes or funny stories, and he did make us laugh. But, this jocularity was actually one of the expressions of dementia, according to Bradley Boeve.

An isolated incident illustrates some of the odd and disturbing things a person with dementia will say. My mother was ill in a nursing home out of state. We knew it was not going to be long before she passed away. On 8 December 2010, I received a call around lunch time saying that she was gone. Wanting to talk to someone, I called Bryan at work, expecting him to say something customary, such as, "I know you will miss her," or something like that. Instead, in a snippy, angry tone of voice he said, "This doesn't mean we have to go to Texas, does it?" Certainly an uncaring comment like that was not what I expected to hear, but it now seems clear evidence of dementia at work.

In the following years, Bryan wrote another book, published in 2012, this time about Betsy's father. For this writing, he had to become even closer to the family. He corresponded with Betsy's siblings as well. Once I even questioned Bryan, saying, "You do know you are not part of their family, don't you?" Sometimes it actually seemed that he was more involved in their lives than in our life together. Everything he did seemed to be done "over the top" – that is, in a way that seemed exaggerated to a normal person.

I kept a diary of the incidences that happened during these years. I will share some of that diary here in order to help the reader visualize and understand the awful, relentless progression of dementia in Bryan's case. During this time period, I wrote the following entry in my diary of events:

> Got up at 11:30 p.m. Felt that I must have heard something, but couldn't be sure. His car was gone. Sat up all night waiting for him. Finally, after 5 a.m., I called, afraid that he wouldn't answer and I would be more worried than I already was. He sounded sleepy and said he'd been called in to

work for an emergency [electrical, I believe] and I should've called earlier instead of worrying. I asked that he please wake me or leave me a note should this happen again.

This is the only time he used his car to leave the house at night. Oh yes, he did begin to sneak out occasionally.

The reader needs to realize that Bryan had always been a faithful husband. Unlike other husbands who make their wives feel jealous by staring at a beautiful woman out in public, Bryan had never done this. He never made me feel inadequate or inferior or embarrassed me with his treatment of another woman. This is why his new behavioral patterns were so clearly the opposite of his true personality.

I can't help but compare Bryan's behavior to that of a teenager, who would think it was great fun to do something "daring" like sneak out of his parents' house at night. An acquaintance told me that when his father had Alzheimer's his father's behavior reverted to that of a "fifteen year old." How many times did I describe Bryan's behavior the same way – dozens, certainly! In the beginning, I thought that Bryan was just being silly and would "grow out" of the behavior, that perhaps he was having a small, late "mid-life crisis," if you will. However, the juvenile nature of this behavior fits right in line with what happens to a person's mind when it is affected by dementia.

Recently, I was speaking with a nurse and she likened Bryan's behavior to that of a young person who becomes resentful of his mother (me) because the babysitter (Betsy) is so much nicer to him and lets him do anything he wants, etc. She indicated that the reason Bryan would revert to such juvenile behavior is that he had to go back further and further into the past to find a place where he was comfortable and could function. This idea has merit and could fit some things Bryan said very well.

Betsy was forced to clean houses and babysit children to supplement her income after her husband left her. Bryan had her begin cleaning our house. (I should take mild satisfaction in the fact that Betsy had to scrub my toilets.) So, every other week, Betsy was in our home cleaning. Bryan began to do odd jobs at Betsy's house "since she had no man to help her." Remember, he was not at all interested in doing anything around his own home. Someone described this as the "white knight syndrome" wherein a man feels better about himself when he is "rescuing a helpless female." Helping his own wife just doesn't give the man the same ego boost, apparently. When asked why he was only helping one person from our religious congregation, Bryan answered that he was "only being a friend."

One day when Betsy came over to the house to clean, she let slip that "men Bryan's age need ____ (mumbling)." When I pressed her for what these men needed, she refused to answer. Of course she couldn't – she would then be revealing to me how she was trying to supply this need for my husband! As I figured out the truth about her behavior, how I wanted to tell her she was unwelcome in my home. I felt I couldn't do so however. I was never certain how Bryan would respond, as his behavior had become unpredictable. I was afraid to do anything that might push him away from me and toward Betsy. It was not worth the risk to kick Betsy out of our home, despite my feelings. It felt awful to me to have to act from the position of fear. Everything in the Scots-Irish part of my heritage rebelled against that! A girl who descends from the "Give 'Em Hell Hendens" shouldn't act in fear, but I desperately wanted to hold my marriage together.

A general diary entry for the whole of 2016 reads:

> She calls him for advice on home projects & computer issues; to babysit her daughter's dogs (many weekends); comes by house for this and that; and is included in almost every event we

attend – from social security seminar free dinners to movies to music events. He is always ready to help her, and makes me feel badly for resenting it, saying it is "being a friend" and that "it's nice to have someone else along who has a different viewpoint." I tell him she is taking advantage of him and he shrugs it off.

By the summer of 2016, it seemed Betsy was invited to every event we attended. When we went to the movies, Bryan would sit in the middle of Betsy and me and talk to her during the movie, leaving me to watch it alone. When we got home and I complained about this, Bryan would tell me that she didn't understand the movie like I was able to, and he had to explain it to her – a strange answer that no one would believe.

Any wife could tell you that this is not normal behavior for a husband. If a man was actually trying to have an affair, he would certainly not be inviting his wife along on assignations with his mistress! No wife enjoys feeling unappreciated, but this is one of the many emotional abuses I suffered during Bryan's years of dementia. It took incredible strength of will, day after day, for me not to force the issue of Betsy's inclusion in our outings and demand we go without her.

I felt Betsy was constantly being thrown in my face and I was not happy about it. It was just such strange behavior for my usually kind husband to be so inconsiderate and not change his behavior even when asked to do so. As the Hospice Social Worker later said, "You can't reason with a drunk," indicating that reasoning with a person with dementia is just as impossible.

Then came the morning when I discovered my husband getting out of Betsy's car at 6:00 a.m.:

12 November 2016 Saturday
Woke up at first light knowing that he was planning to leave for Monroe air show early. It was time he should be up, so went to check. He was not in the house. Walked down driveway to edge of house, where I could see down road. Saw him get out of a mid-size silver car, parked in the middle of the street just forward of the curve in the road, and trot toward our house.

When he approached up the driveway, I said, "What on earth are you doing?" He mumbled that he "had planned to be back before this" and pushed past me into the house. When I followed him inside, he said that he had met her to give her a jacket he had bought and some patches so that she could sew them on before the hangar dance that night so he could wear it. He had not wanted to tell me he'd bought something else (although he said he only paid $12 for the jacket). Then he went to take a shower.

As he was leaving the house for the show, I asked again if he had any more to tell me, that she would have pulled up in the driveway, surely, not dropped him off down the road like that if what he had said was true. He turned completely cold – like I have never seen him before. I followed him out to the car; he said he was "tired of our marriage." I began to cry. He said he had to go and drove away.

Approximately 1 p.m., he texted me and asked how sales were going (I had a book table at a local museum) like everything was OK and he didn't remember anything about the morning. I sat at the museum all day shivering and shaking, numb with anxiety.

Yes, Bryan texted me at 1 p.m. the day of the air show and asked how my sales were going at the book signing table that I had that day at a local museum. This is an important thing to note about dementia. Bryan acted as if *nothing had happened* that morning, as if he had completely forgotten everything. No apology, no explanation, nothing. It was more than strange, but very typical behavior for a person with dementia, where **memory becomes selective**. (Cerebral Function Unit, UK, bold mine.)

One thing that needs explaining. On the Saturday of the air show: *I was not allowed to attend*. Yes, in the twenty-first century, my husband told me he didn't want me there, and I didn't go. On Sunday, I could go with him and that was fine, but on Saturday, he attended the hangar dance after the show, and he wanted to "live out a fantasy" without me there. Yes, those where his actual words, heard from his own lips when we were refueling our car after attending a meeting for air show volunteers. When I later mentioned the word "fantasy" he did not remember what I was talking about. He was not trying to fool me, he honestly didn't remember. His voice took on a certain timbre when he was lying, and so I could recognize when he was avoiding the truth. As a dutiful (and irritated) wife, I did go and sit in the back to see how he behaved at the hangar dance and he did nothing untoward in public there. Surely no man who was trying to have an actual affair would let his wife see him going about it this way! His behavior just seemed so bizarre.

When dressing up in re-enacting clothes, Bryan had

the chance to become a person he had never been – an outgoing one. He really *was* living out a fantasy; one that only dementia let him have the courage to live out. Without the loss of inhibition that losing gray matter from his frontal lobe provided, Bryan could never have acted the way he did as it was completely against his normal quiet nature. At this time, he also took up some public speaking, although one could tell it was way out of his comfort zone as a quiet person and his first few speeches were painful to watch.

There is a curious thing about dementia. Bryan seemed to phase in and out of the dementia so that it was hard to tell what he would say next. He said a cruel thing like being tired of me that one morning, yet he often called me "sweetie" and shared my love for our WWII veterans, which made him feel worthwhile and bonded us together.

He had to come up with explanations for some things he said, and sometimes the explanation did not come until the next day, when he had time to think about it, but he was always trying to ensure that I didn't "kick him out of the house," as it were. The "real" Bryan did not want to leave me, and had no intention of doing so. The confused "dementia mind" just knew he needed help to feel like himself again.

During 2017, Bryan snuck out of the house at night several times. It was as if he was a teenager again and doing the things he had been too shy to do back when he actually was one. When questioned, he admitted that he had spent time "nursing a coke" at a karaoke restaurant/bar down the road. Then he said that he sat in front of a hamburger place whose drive-in stayed open late, talking on the phone to Betsy, but that they weren't together. Most women would not believe such a story, of course. However, one part of such a curious story could actually be in character with his normal mind, not just his "dementia mind." As strange as it sounds, "nursing a coke" so he wouldn't have to spend much money is exactly like something he would do. He seems not to have taken to drinking alcohol, which in his right mind he abhorred. That is fortunate, because drinking would have made his walking at night even more dangerous.

The following incident displays how dementia makes one distrustful of everyone. Bryan told many falsehoods during his years with dementia, even including a lie to his supervisor at work that I found out about. I have a feeling that there were many more lies about which I never heard:

19 August 2017   Saturday

On Monday he said that he needed to go camping and fishing at a local camping area "sooner rather than later," even though it was 90-something degrees. On Saturday, he loaded his little car full of camping & fishing gear. Before 4 p.m. I called to tell him I had checked on his camping reservation and they didn't have one for him. He said he usually just snuck in and they never checked. I felt funny about this, so I decided to drive over to his facility and use a desire to "get an extra hug goodbye" as my excuse. When I got there at 4:30, his car was not there, and his boss said he had left at 4 p.m. He had told his boss that he and I had an event to go to and that's why he needed to leave early. The boss promised not to let on that I had come by.

He left his phone there at the facility, but I had given him the other phone in case it had a better signal while he was camping. He called me on it at 5:30, saying he "decided to call me on this phone," and he was going out to his car to leave. Of course, I was driving home from the facility when he did so, so he was caught in the lie, but I didn't let on.

The anxiety shown by Bryan in feeling that he needed to get away from something *now* could also be related to dementia. Under normal conditions, he would never have wanted to go camping during a time of the year with such high temperatures. The fact that he lied to his supervisor when it was unnecessary is also disturbing. He could have gotten off early without making up an untruthful excuse. However, a person with more advanced dementia doesn't see lying as a wrongful behavior anymore.

> Lying may occur at any stage but more generally in the mid-to-late stage [of dementia].
> (Home Care Assistance Jefferson County.)

Bryan was in a motorcycle accident a few days later; hit by a car from behind while he was waiting at a red light. He had facial surgery that night after the accident and his broken wrist was fixed a few days later. The CT scan of his head showed how far his dementia had progressed at that point – already approximately twenty years older than his actual age. But – I was not informed of the results of this scan at that time, so I still didn't know the reason for Bryan's behavior.

At one point in this journey, Betsy turned on an old cell phone, paying for it on her own account, and gave it to Bryan so they could talk privately at night. Many are the nights I spent standing in my hallway listening to my husband's part of the conversation. Bryan went to great lengths to try to keep these phones hidden from me, as shown in this almost humorous example:

29 November 2017 Wednesday

He put up rope lights on the deck this morning. We needed one more strand and I left for Old Time Pottery, just down the road, to get it. When I returned, I assumed he had heard me drive up & enter the house, but he had not. He was sitting on the deck talking on a phone. I saw the phone clearly because the chair was facing outward toward the yard and his back was to me. He was using the speaker phone and thus was holding the phone out in front of him. It was a very old phone that he says he uses for "music" because it "has good speakers." I have indeed seen him play music on it when mowing the yard.

 The phone obviously had a signal. When I opened the sliding glass door onto the deck, he quickly tried to hide it from me, a very clumsy attempt of fumbling around so he could get it hung up. I heard him say to her, "We'll talk about that later." And to me he said, "Did you get the rope light?" – very loudly – hoping no doubt to let her know that I was there. Then he even went so far as to call her back, using his regular phone, of course. All I said to him was that he didn't have to hang up in the first place.

His mishandling of the phone was funny, of course, but it was not so funny that Betsy had agreed to go behind my back to talk privately with my husband. She was willing to go along with inappropriate behavior and even sanction it by spending money to do it.

Sadly, just as if my life was a novel, "the plot thickened":

30 November 2017 Thursday
He must have been worried I had seen the phone, because when I said, "So, you were able to get new music on your phone the other day. I've still never listened to those speakers, although I remember reading on the internet that they were very good," he replied that it was in his bag (in which he takes his lunch and things to work) in the kitchen, and I was welcome to listen. He has never said that before. When he went to watch Thursday night football, I did get it out of the bag and of course it had no signal.

This meant he was actually worried that I knew about the phone and the two of them colluded together to cut off the signal and cut it back on again. Therefore, there is no way that Betsy could not have known that Bryan was trying to hide the phone from me.

This also means there is no way she could not have known that what she was doing was morally wrong: interfering in someone else's marriage and trying to ingratiate herself between the two parties in the marriage.

I had to repeat the following scenario over and over again, as Betsy kept supplying Bryan with new cell phones or new numbers. This forced me into a position of being sneaky myself:

2 December 2017   Saturday
He left the phone on his bedside table while taking a shower, so I snatched it up and went in other room and called my cell phone on it. It rang through. Now I have saved the number to the phone on my cell, being careful to delete the call on his phone, of course.

Once I was brave enough to question Bryan about his behavior. He gave me a strange answer: "I didn't think you would mind." Of course, anyone who was thinking correctly would have understood why I was upset about his talking "privately" with another woman at night. However, Bryan's answer shows how his thinking was distorted, and with his inhibitions dropping away due to the loss of brain matter in his frontal lobe, he no longer understood why anyone would think his behavior was inappropriate. This also seems to prove what the nurse told me about becoming the "mother figure" instead of his wife in his mind.

The time before I discovered what was wrong with Bryan's mind was the most agonizing time of my life. The whole foundation of what I believed and depended upon in life was shattered. At times he almost appeared to hate me. At other times, he treated me as if I had no feelings at all. But then at other times, he seemed his normal self and could make a kind gesture. It was certainly a very confusing time. On top of this, he was convinced that a very manipulating woman was a good person, one to be put on a pedestal. In his dementia mind, he actually thought everyone could see this and that it was the truth, as his surprise when someone else didn't agree proved. In his shrinking mind, he thought he was idolizing and helping a person worthy of that help. The truth was that Betsy was certainly not acting as a person of noble character who deserved to be idolized.

The following diary excerpt will illustrate an example of the ridiculous situations that can happen to a family in which a member has dementia – especially if that family member picks someone like Betsy to befriend. (Note to the reader: in this diary entry I was quite blunt about how Betsy was dressed that evening. I decided not to delete the statement in an effort for the reader to visualize how upset I really felt.)

16 December 2017 Saturday
Military Order of the Purple Heart Christmas dinner at 6 p.m. She arrived late. Compared to the other conservatively-dressed wives there, who were wearing a Christmas sweater and pants or a skirt, she was dressed like a "hooker," with over-the knee boots and a short, very tight dress. She and another friend, whom I had invited as a buffer from having to talk to her, sat across from B and me. Bryan and she acted like they hardly knew each other – very circumspect. Only one time did I notice anything unusual. He appeared to be trying to mouth something to her privately. I bumped his leg and that stopped it, and he tried to cover up by repeating something she had said previously, like

that was what he was trying to ask.

On our way home, she was driving behind us. She called first his phone, which he could not get out of his pocket to answer, then my phone. She sounded upset and said her car was acting funny – jerky and hesitant – and would we wait for her somewhere. At the time, there were five police cars speeding by and we didn't know what was up ahead. She noticed then that she had left the parking brake on. That should have taken care of it, but she still wanted us to stop. I told her we would pull off at the QT on the next corner. I told B to pull under a light away from the pumps.

When she pulled in, I got out of the car as well, in order to give them no chance to talk. He told her to push down and release the brake a couple of times. He sounded "tired" about the incident, which was a rather obvious stunt. Imagine an almost-seventy-year-old supposedly mature woman acting this way with another woman's husband – and right in front of the wife! How blatant!

The following entry was from the next week in December:

22 December 2017   Friday

He told me tonight in the car on the way to the Southpark Mall area that his good friend from Texas, with whom he has taken many hiking trips, had called him today and told him he has cancer. Naturally, Bryan was sad about this.

While watching the skaters at the ice rink at Southpark, he was very distant, didn't look at me, and didn't appear to care what I said. He said he was so tired all the time and working another five years seemed like too much some days. [Rational Thinking Loss #3 probably played a part in his statement here. Keeping his job must have been tremendously hard, as he became unable to follow sequences.]

I woke up abruptly at 3 a.m. and just knew he was gone. Sure enough, he had left a note, saying he had gone for a walk. I decided to wait up to see when he came home. Not to confront, just to see what time, and if I could see him getting out of a car down the road. I sat by the dining room window, all the way against the wall, trying to see down the road. I never saw a car's headlights come down the road. I never saw him walking up. Suddenly, I heard the kitchen door opening. I sat motionless. He gave a big sigh and went down the hall. I waited a while until I thought it was safe and lay down on the couch for the rest of the morning until he got up. I made the excuse to him I had slept part of the night there because I had a coughing spell and thought I needed to sit up more. Both of us were sick with bronchitis (me) and pneumonia (him) so this was reasonable. I did not mention seeing him come in. He must have been worried that I had seen him, because he sounded funny when he talked to me, asking "How's your bronchitis?" instead of saying, "How are you feeling?"

In the above entry, when I described how "he was very distant, didn't look at me, and didn't appear to care what I said," I was describing the very essence of the lack of empathy and lack of emotion that comes with dementia.

In this entry, Bryan seemed to be trying to get rid of Betsy, but she wasn't going to go away, as the next two entries prove:

26 December 2017 Tuesday
Saw the film *Last Jedi* at 8:10 p.m. showing, so it was after 11 p.m. when we got home. He went right

to bed, pleading a headache from the cold. (He had mentioned "almost having a headache" earlier in the day.) He said he would be fine when left alone in the dark room. I went to my office computer and then I heard him talking on the phone. He was talking very softly and I could not hear every word, even though I tiptoed all the way down until I could touch the doorframe of the door. I made out these distinct phrases:

    1. "It is just not going to work like this."
    2. "I know it will hurt."
    3. "We have to stop the risky behavior."

[Note: he stopped leaving the house at night after this conversation.]

In order for Betsy to feel hurt about the behavior that was going to be stopped, she had to be participating in the behavior willingly. Notice in this next diary entry how insistent she had become about feeling that she had a *right* to be part of Bryan's life:

27 December 2017 Wednesday
Of all things, she called me on my cell phone about 8 p.m. this evening. I took it into another room away from him when I saw it was her calling. She asked

to come over to the house because she had a gift for him for his last time keeping the dogs that she had never given him. I just said that it would not be convenient. No explanation. She said "oh" rather suprisedly and fumbled with some other sentence and I just repeated, "No, tonight would not be convenient." She said maybe some other time and we hung up.

Then he and I decided on the spur of the moment to go to Buffalo Wild Wings and watch the Texas Bowl, in which my nephew played. We stayed for the whole game, not getting home until 1 a.m. This is unheard of for us to stay out so late.

31 December 2017   Sunday
Attended religious congregation for New Year's Eve and was enjoying a time of worship. At approximately ten minutes to midnight, she showed up, wearing a long, blue, shimmering evening gown. She had obviously been at a dance that would have lasted through the countdown to 2018, yet she left early to come to congregation for the countdown. [Congregants stood in a circle, holding hands and praying up until the stroke of midnight.] During the New Year's Kiss, he held me way off,

stiffly, at full arm's length, presumably because she was watching from the other side of the circle. He spoke to her briefly, then we left.

This would be the last time we attended our religious congregation. These entries demonstrate how difficult my life was for the last few years of Bryan's life. I had to stay up late to listen to phone conversations and to see if he sneaked out of the house. I suffered intense emotional abuse because of his behavior and because Betsy would not leave him alone. I would have suffered less if she had had the courtesy to honor my husband's marriage vows.

According to the beliefs of our religious congregation, her behavior was called "adultery" no matter what Bryan said to her or if they were physical or not. The intention to dishonor Bryan's marriage vows was there on her part, regardless, as her brain was not clouded by dementia.

I had to try to keep her apart from my husband to the best of my ability. I asked for help from a leading woman in the congregation – if she would speak to Betsy on my behalf – but I never received any help. It is unfortunate that this set of circumstances prevented us from attending our religious congregation, which denied me the comfort that attendance there would have provided. I have to admit I felt very let down.

With this next entry, my life reached a real low point. Remember, eleven years previous, when Bryan published his first book, he listed on the dedication page that I was his "bride and soul mate" – even after thirty years of marriage! Read what he said in 2018 that explains why I came to dislike the phrase, "soul mate":

29 January 2018   Monday
This night he professed his love for her, as his "soul mate." He "cried all day Friday and Saturday" one week when he thought she had found someone else. (Funny, I don't remember him crying.)

He told her that even if she died, he "would never pursue another woman."

The really bad part of the conversation was obviously about me: "She has belittled, ridiculed, and manipulated me. I don't trust a thing she says. That bond of trust has been broken and can never be fixed." He said the words adamantly and vehemently. He came across as being desperate – so over-the-top clingy. The words themselves were interesting: I had used "belittled and ridiculed" in a sentence about something else just a few days before, so he was parroting what I had said. In a note of irony, accusing me of manipulating him was a telling choice of words, because he was so obviously trying to manipulate her.

At one point, he also reassured her that, while I "might think this trip [to Charleston, planned for the end of March] is going to change things," it won't change his feelings for her. (Funny, right before he had this conversation, he had told me that he had gotten the Saturday off for the trip approved at work, and was pleased about it and looking forward to it.)

Altogether a stunning, disturbing, disheartening conversation for me to overhear.

If nothing else, this disturbing conversation proves that Bryan spoke to Betsy out of his "dementia mind," not his real mind. He said how he truly felt about the upcoming trip, and then told her right afterwards that she was so important to him that he cried all day for two days when he thought she might have found someone else. No wise woman would believe a typical *line* such as that one was! It sounded more like something from an old movie than something that someone would actually say. This sounds like one of the "stereotyped behaviors" that were mentioned earlier in the introduction to this section.

One would assume that surely Betsy had to realize that he was just saying anything to her to convince her to keep speaking with him and that he didn't really mean the actual words. *Except* – she apparently believed every word, which I discovered when she perpetrated a cruel, unfeelingly incident in our religious congregation's parking lot four months after Bryan died. The words she spoke at that time – actually an admission of guilt on her part, although she didn't realize it – convinced me that, sadly, she really did believe what he said.

That morning, 29 August 2020, I got out of my vehicle and began walking to the front door of the religious building. Suddenly, a car wheeled around in front of me and pulled up alongside me. Betsy began to yell at me, accusing me of something that sounded like I had "called her names."

I glanced at her face for around two seconds. It was a face so distorted by what appeared to be hatred, or perhaps actual evil, that I couldn't stand to look at it. I just looked down at her tires to see which way they were turned and kept walking towards the building. She screamed that I *"would* stop and talk" to her, but I did not do so.

Then she stated her admission of guilt: "Get this

through your head; I didn't come between you. You destroyed your marriage all by yourself." Naturally, this was an awful thing to say to a new widow who had devoted herself to her husband's care. Betsy appeared to be filled with bitterness and unkindness. She displayed no concern for my pain and grief as a new widow – far from it! She was actually defending her position as the adulteress, as if she was in the right and I was in the wrong.

By now, I had walked almost to the plaza area at the front door of the building. Betsy hurled one last thing at me: she threatened me with a restraining order to keep me from attending the religious congregation. "And you know I'll do it too!" she cried out. Even at the time, when I was only concerned with my safety as she seemed so unhinged and unpredictable that morning (I was on foot and she had her car which she could use as a weapon against me), this threat sounded extremely ludicrous, almost funny – a totally hollow threat.

Despite its unpleasantness, this incident was useful to me in that it caused me to discover Betsy's Instagram username – her and my husband's initials – as shown in this diary entry:

30 August 2020
"(her initials)andbbforever"

Imagine her having the gall to put something like that out over the internet, linking her name with *another woman's husband*. Most people would consider this shameful behavior, but apparently she did not consider it to be so. It is as childish a thing to do as things Bryan did – but he had dementia as an excuse!

Of course, in those last years of his life, I had a hard time dealing with hearing Bryan say inappropriate things to another woman. Because of his dementia, Bryan somehow needed to feel he was "pursuing" another woman – something he didn't really do in his youth – and to him it didn't matter how that felt for me because he couldn't reason it out anymore. (Rational Thinking Losses #1 and #2.) I cried many tears into my pillow during all these years, not knowing why my husband had turned against me.

My goal became just to keep my marriage together. I wanted to somehow prevent him from doing something that would destroy all our years together. So, I put up with a good deal of abuse. It was extremely hard on me – how often I wished I could lash out in anger – but I felt I had no choice but to keep my integrity, honor my marriage vows, and endure, trying to remember the good times in the first thirty-something years of our marriage, times in which we were a couple that no one could have separated.

I saw a counselor three times during the early part of 2018. I felt this counselor was only encouraging me to leave my husband, and so I discontinued going. Here is a letter I sent to the counselor. It very well describes my feelings at the time. It's actually hard for me to read how upset I was back then. But I was a woman whose world had fallen apart:

Dear [Counselor's name]:

I was disappointed in our last session because I didn't feel I got anything that I could really use to help me deal with all this. I don't know how to "Lean into my marriage" when the other person obviously doesn't love me and doesn't want to share any thoughts with me. We watch the TV shows that he likes. That is it. That is all there is to "lean into."

I have spent the last week depressed and angry, reliving how he has treated me for the last several years. He spent that time belittling me, mocking me, etc. He constantly threw the other woman in my face and made me live with the seething humiliation.

He cared absolutely nothing for my feelings and never listened when I complained about her constant presence. He obviously had no qualms about leaving me alone in the house all night, with me not knowing I was unprotected. He has lied to me many times and even lied to his boss at least once. He gave all his affections to her, leaving nothing for me and made it very obvious by actually shying away from my touch a few times.

How can I respect a man of such low moral character?

Let's face it: he wants a Stepford wife. As long as I smile nicely and give him his dinner and don't voice any complaints, or try to have an in-depth conversation, or express any of my feelings, he is OK.

I feel extremely resentful. All I have had is sorrow and terror and anxiety and anger. The man has completely destroyed my life. All I believed in is gone. How will I ever trust anyone again? And why should I want to?

When, if ever, will I have any hopes and dreams again? When will I even be able to enjoy anything again??? When will I be able to smile and actually mean it, not just pretend? Living the rest of my life without love is a depressing prospect.

It does no good to hear statistics that say 40-50% of marriages suffer from infidelity. It does no good to think of all the women in history who have lived with husbands that they knew were not faithful. This man has broken our bond of trust and there is no way to forget that. My whole life was built on this bond and now I don't know how to live or how to think.

This is what I need help dealing with. Encouraging me to leave is not helpful. The pain would still be there. Telling me to lean into nothing is not helpful. Do you have anything to help me?

This counselor couldn't help me, but I did have a friend from another state who gave me some encouragement. I am listing first the email I sent her (this email gives another synopsis of what I had been through) and then her reply:

May 4, 2018 [to friend]

Some days I seem better and others not so good. I have trouble remembering things in conversation – but only with him. I suppose it is because I am so preoccupied all the time. I wish I could just forget about it, but I cannot. It fills most of my days and nights. When I begin to think of how he would have treated a family dog better than he has me, then I become angry and just about forget what I am trying to do – survive.

It might have been different if he had some one-night stands when on a business trip or something like that. What he did was so *planned*, and he just threw it right in my face over and over. There was no doubt that he preferred another woman over me and I knew exactly who it was. He yelled at me and his voice got soft when he spoke of her. He invited her to go almost everywhere we went – the three of us together. He sat between us in the movies and talked to her, leaving me sitting there. He did everything to let me know that I was not loved anymore, including not saying it and not touching me.

He walked right out of the house at exactly 11:30 at night and came home between 5 and 5:30 a.m., leaving a note saying he had gone for a walk. He talked to her on a cell phone after he went to bed at night for thirty minutes to an hour most nights, on a phone she is paying for.

The sneaking out and phone calls went on

for over a year and a half. The going everywhere with us was the previous year. When he started sneaking out, he pretty much quit asking her to come with us. We still, however, go over and feed her daughter's dogs when she goes out of town – twice this spring. He does not go to her house to fix things anymore, and she does not call to ask a million questions about the computer, etc, like she used to. She was still doing this after he started sneaking out, however, for a good while. It has been four months since he has left the house and several weeks since he has had a nighttime conversation with her [this was after our trip to Charleston] – all good signs.

So, I should be happy that he is taking me places. However, I am not really happy because the hurt is just too much. Most of the time, the hurt is all I can think of. I feel then that I will never be OK again.

I do have an appointment with a pastoral counselor at a church on the 17th. That seems so far away. I have to try to hold on until then and see if this gentleman feels I should say anything to B, but it is so hard. All I want to do is say something. I believe all these people who are advising me that I have to keep quiet and let it slide just have never been here and don't know what they are asking. Everything in me wants justice – except that there is no justice to be had. Even if he should apologize – which he will never do – he could not erase my memory of what he did. Nothing can do that, and some days living is just so hard to do.

May 4, 2018 [from friend to me]

I don't really think betrayal of any kind is ever acceptable or [that] the kind or duration makes much difference. And, unless you are a one in a hundred million who can totally forget and forgive, you can "glue" life back together but the cracks will always show. It might be a little bit of a relief if you had the option of just yelling, hitting, biting and kicking shins but that really wouldn't fix it completely. I think you are extremely strong to keep all of the distasteful feelings inside and not let it show. I am afraid I would not be able to do that. I cannot believe that he thinks you don't know anything about what he was doing but you have borne up under it all with such dignity.

I am glad you have an appointment to see a counselor. Just having someone to listen who hopefully is not biased is a great help in facing every day. It is said that life is not particularly about what happens to you but what you do about what happens to you. You have proven yourself to be of very strong mind and character and anyone should be proud to know you and be called your friend. I sure do and I surely do admire you.

Please remember that the letter and the emails were all written expressing my true feelings and *before* I knew that Bryan had dementia; *before* I had any explanation for his behavior.

The letter and emails do show some more points about dementia that are only now clear in hindsight:

1. **"He cared absolutely nothing for my feelings and never listened when I complained about her constant presence."** The lack of empathy that a dementia patient develops is very obvious in this statement I made. He also likely couldn't follow my arguments when I would complain about her presence.

2. **"actually shying away from my touch a few times."** Only recently did I hear another wife whose husband has dementia talk about her husband not wanting to be touched and becoming agitated when she tried to touch him. It was comforting to hear that it was not just my touch

that was not wanted, but any touch.

3. "As long as I smile nicely and give him his dinner and don't voice any complaints, or try to have an in-depth conversation, or express any of my feelings, he is OK." I can see now that this is all he *could* do. He wasn't capable of in-depth conversation or dealing with feelings. If I just "smiled nicely" and didn't pressure him for anything more, he could relax because no one was asking him to do that which he was no longer able to do.

4. "My whole life was built on this bond and now I don't know how to live or how to think." "Most of the time, the hurt is all I can think of. I feel then that I will never be OK again. These sentences surely show my desperation at the time and were hard for me to read now. In three years, I had almost forgotten the intensity of the pain.

However, there *were* some comical moments during this miserable time:

> An evening somewhere in 2018
> When he got up from the couch during this evening, his black phone [the one Betsy was paying for] dropped out of his pocket and fell on the floor. The back came off and the battery came out. It landed upside down. He said something about the phone

being slippery and left the room. When he came back he made a show of pretending to attach the back of his regular phone securely. It was actually comical.

6 March 2018   Tuesday

He called her. We had had such a nice evening, it made me just plain angry that he was talking to her, so I did what the counselor said. [I saw a counselor three times during this period.] I went down and heated up my neck warmer sock and when I went down the hall, I pushed the door open and asked was he awake and did he call me: "I thought I heard you say something." I could see absolutely nothing, as it was so dark. He made a big deal about how he was coughing and he drank some water. I asked if he needed anything and he said no. I waited by the door, but never heard him call her back. He continued to cough though, which was only justice.

Bryan had some moments when he was in his real mind and when he actually spoke true words to the problem of Betsy. One evening something Bryan said indicated that Betsy was not that "sensible" a person – I do not remember what was said exactly. He continued by saying that it would indeed "be hard to put up with her all the time." At least this tells me that while in his right mind, he would certainly not have left me for her. There's a little comfort in that, I suppose.

In October of 2018, I discovered the old cell phone was turned back on, even though it had been turned off in May as he had promised it would be. We had an unpleasant conversation. The next day, however, he was so nice – very talkative and pleasant as we drove to Greenville, South Carolina to see World War II bomber aircraft. Was the "real" Bryan there for a few hours? Perhaps knowing he had said something wrong the previous day, but not remembering what it was? It was hard for me to tell, so I tried to enjoy what I could about the day, all the while having that sick feeling in my stomach that had come to stay.

Our Cancer Journey

Things were relatively quiet in the spring of 2019, and then in August of 2019, Bryan was diagnosed with bladder cancer. During July, he had been treated for urinary tract infections. When the pain continued, his doctor finally sent him for a CT scan of his abdomen, which showed a large cancerous tumor in his bladder.

A nephrostomy tube was put in Bryan's left kidney, which was blocked from draining by the tumor. He spent a couple of nights in the hospital. His surgeon deemed the cancer non-resectable, and his PET scan showed that there was cancer in four lymph nodes around the bladder, but nowhere else.

The radiation treatments began on 26 August and continued every weekday for three weeks. After the first two weeks, his intestinal tract was never the same. He may have also been a little more tired than usual, but otherwise there were no other symptoms.

The 17th of September saw his first chemotherapy

treatment, using two drugs, with the second treatment, this time with only one of the drugs, on the 24th. October 8 and 15 were the next two treatments, with the next two on the 22nd and 29th. Unbelievably, he was still working during October.

All during treatment, he continued to eat. Food still tasted good to him, and he had no trouble with vomiting. He took anti-nausea medicine only a few times, and that was preventative.

That fall, I was confident that we could beat the cancer. I tried to keep upbeat, and to be an encouragement to Bryan.

On 5 November he had a chemo treatment, but on the 22nd was treated for an unexplained fever. By the 24th of November, he was using a cane to walk. He had the last chemo treatments on 3 and 10 December. On 6 December, he quit working due to shakiness and dizziness. He also stopped driving and I took him to all his appointments. I had been accompanying him anyway, so I could hear what the doctors said and address any issues I saw.

Bryan had a PET scan on 13 December and the results were great. The cancer had shrunk back down into the bladder. We saw a new surgeon on the 31st and surgery to remove the bladder was now back on the table, as it were.

The surgeon had a nephrostomy tube put in Bryan's right kidney on the second of January in an effort to save kidney function. Bryan spent one night in the hospital, although it seemed unnecessary.

Around this time, I mailed a letter to Betsy, my first attempt to contact her in a long while. The letter asked her to please leave Bryan alone and to let us have peace. The letter did no good at all. She completely ignored this plea from a wife and continued to be in his life. It's so hard for me to understand this – she knew what it felt like to have an unfaithful husband. Why would she want to do the same to another woman?

During the rest of January, Bryan developed a compulsive behavior. Even though his kidneys were draining into the tubes in his back, he still felt the need to hurry to the bathroom twenty times a day. Getting up so many times during the day and night seemed to be way out of proportion to any actual need. I feel this compulsive behavior was perhaps a symptom of his dementia.

On the morning of the 29th of January, Bryan underwent surgery to remove his bladder. When the surgeon got inside, he discovered the PET scan had not given the whole picture, and he was unable to remove anything – Bryan woke up with all the cancer still in him, a crushing blow. (He did receive an ileostomy and the tubes in his back were removed.) However, I still didn't give up hope, and tried to keep Bryan from doing so either.

The hospital stay was quite lengthy this time: seventeen days. Some of that time was needed to "wake up" Bryan's intestinal tract, so he spent days eating nothing but ice chips. This seemed to set him up for failure to start eating again. By the time there was no medical reason to keep him in hospital any longer, I had visited several nursing facilities and gotten Bryan admitted to the nicest rehabilitation program in our city.

Bryan had been there almost a week when he started behaving very oddly. I was in his room, talking on the phone and transacting some business that needed to be taken care of, and when I got off the phone, I noticed Bryan was holding the remote control for the TV remarkably like one would hold a phone up to one's ear. He held it out to me, saying, "I have been on hold a long time, would you take this?" My shock must have shown on my face. Soon, he was back in the hospital for another five days, fighting a urinary tract infection.

The rehabilitation facility took him back for another whole two weeks, in which time he grew stronger physically, but not mentally. He began to say that he was tired of "institutional food" and began refusing to eat anything. The facility offered a free meal each day to a family member and so I had lunch with him most every day (occasionally dinner). I was eating the food and enjoying it. There seemed no good reason but stubbornness – or rather, dementia – that Bryan would not eat. When the personnel there tried to get him to go to the dining room for meals, he carried on so terribly that it was embarrassing and I requested that he be served in his room again. When we merely went past the dining room toward the physical therapy room, he would hold his nose and wave his arms around. This behavior was so child-like. He was no longer acting like a teenager in these instances, but pouting like a much younger child.

Bryan began experiencing anxiety at around 5:00 p.m. every day after he returned home from rehab. I thought this looked like remarkably like sundowning, so I requested an anti-depressant for him, which worked quickly and stopped the symptoms. Sundowning, of course, is a major late-stage Alzheimer's symptom. During the spring of 2020, Bryan exhibited all the common symptoms of Alzheimer's disease but one – he still had the ability to swallow – although he didn't want to eat.

When Bryan got home, he could stand without being so shaky, thanks to rehab workouts, but he still refused to eat. I made milkshakes out of meal replacement drinks, as the hospital suggested. These would have given him over 2,000 calories a day, and I was hoping to keep him going on this. After another hospital stay of a week and a half, during which time I was unable to visit due to the covid-19 virus scare, and which encompassed our 43rd anniversary, he came home refusing anything but a plain meal replacement drink, saying that the milkshakes were too thick. This put him dangerously close to being unable to swallow – the last Alzheimer's symptom he didn't yet have.

During this time he also began to exhibit another compulsive behavior. Just like before, he would get up twenty times a day to go to the bathroom. I covered him with three blankets – he was so cold – over and over and over, as I watched him become weaker and weaker, made worse by getting up so much. He used a walker after his surgery and never graduated back to a cane.

Even as his condition became progressively worse, Bryan refused to talk about anything important and left no instructions about how he wanted things to be handled after he was gone. Late-stage cancer combined with what looked like late-stage dementia prevented him from leaving any real last words.

During his last days at home, Bryan didn't talk very much at all. He was so tired, everything was an effort. One day I tried to briefly recount how far we had come on the cancer journey, hoping that he might want to talk about things. His response was typical for a dementia patient: "I don't care what you have done for me." Wounding words, if one lets them be so.

Also, during his last days at home, Betsy was actively trying to be part of his life. I became very angry that Betsy would manifest herself in his life when we were going through such a difficult time – our last days together!

11 April 2020   Saturday

I got B to go out onto the deck. The sun was bright and I could see him squinting, so I went in the house for his sunglasses. They were not where I expected them to be, and I looked in the bathroom, and finally the bedroom I had made up for his return home from the hospital. I still did not see them, so I opened the shallow storage bin in the arm of the recliner in that room. There was a phone being charged in there. I picked it up and it had a signal on it. I hid it and went back outside. Later when he was asleep, I took the phone and a hammer outside and did what I had wanted to do for years – I smashed the phone to bits. It was FUN!

17 April 2020   Friday

While palliative care nurse practitioner was here, from 10 a.m. to 12 p.m., B got up to go to the bathroom. There in his chair was a phone. I picked it up and hid it in my desk. Later when B was asleep, I took it outside and got the phone number off it. Only one call, to her, on the previous day, Thursday. I smashed this phone as well.

He was only home for twelve days before I found him on the floor and figured he had fallen from an incoherent moment due to another urinary tract infection, which turned out to be correct. I took him back to the hospital thinking I had discovered the infection quickly and I would have him back home soon. It was not to be.

I did not give up hope in Bryan's eventual recovery until I was forced to – that was when a Palliative nurse asked me if I wanted them to resuscitate him, breaking a few ribs in the process, and awaken him to more misery than before. Of course, the only possible answer was "no," and the Do Not Resuscitate band was put on his arm. I don't believe he even knew it was there.

On the following morning, Tuesday, a palliative nurse called to tell me that I could visit Bryan with no restrictions and she read to me everything that had been entered on Bryan's chart since I brought him in at 9 p.m. Saturday night. The last thing she said was, "And the generalized brain shrinkage…" I interrupted her: "Back that up! We've never heard this before!"

She continued, "Well, this would be vascular." I answered her, "I understand a little of what you're talking about. My Mom died of vascular Alzheimer's."

I was completely stunned. As I have discovered since then, I was given a gift in receiving this knowledge. It has taken a long time, but I have been able to put my husband's behavior alongside the medical information and see what really happened to him – and thus I wrote this book.

His stay in a Hospice room at the hospital was short – only four days. On Wednesday, the day before his morphine had to be increased, he spoke what were to be the last words of his "dementia mind." These words were so awful, including the words, "I'd rather be dead," that I ran out of the room crying. The next morning the Hospice Social Worker called and told me that I didn't have to come to the hospital and accept such abuse. He said no one would think any less of me if I had to protect myself by not visiting. His words encouraged me greatly, and I did go back to the hospital.

The day before the sad incident above (Tuesday),

however, I was fortunate enough to see the *real* Bryan for a minute and hear his *real* last words. Still stunned by the news of the loss of gray matter in his brain, I was sitting by his bedside, teary-eyed and holding his hand. I cried out to him, "If only I could hear you say one more time that you enjoyed our life together!" I felt this way, of course, because he never seemed to enjoy my company in the last few years. I thought he was asleep, but instead he responded that he had "enjoyed tremendously" our years together and that he had always loved me. It really helped me to hear that. I consider it a gift from above in the midst of a terrible situation – a gift that I can cling to in the years to come.

Bryan's declaration of how much our life together meant to him also made plain the difference between the real person and his "dementia mind." The "real" Bryan still loved me and I would have had no reason to doubt this fact if he had not developed a cruel disease. Yes, Bryan said and did things that were inappropriate and hurtful during the course of his battle with dementia and cancer, but those words and actions came straight from the "dementia mind," not from his heart. He was just a victim of a terrible degenerative disease that was slowly eroding his mind and another that was taking over his body.

On what would turn out to be Bryan's last Sunday

afternoon, I let all of his immediate family call in and say something to him. I was warmed by their heartfelt appreciation. When I was in such a low place, I didn't feel it was possible for me to do something for others. It was nice to know that I could.

That evening, I was warned by a Hospice nurse that she didn't expect Bryan to last more than twenty-four hours. After 2:00 a.m. on 27 April, 2020, I heard his breathing change and become calmer. I got up from the room's recliner and sat in the chair beside his bed and held his hand. At exactly 2:28 a.m., he took a calm breath – and then another one never came.

It was the most surreal experience I have ever had in my life. The hospital was quiet. The room was dark except for the light from the machine supplying his morphine and the small TV that was playing the relaxing soft music that I had had on since he came into the Hospice room. It absolutely felt to me that I was not actually in that room and that this certainly was not my husband in the bed. I don't know another way to explain it.

I sat with him while the nurses pronounced him gone and for another two hours after that, when I was informed that the cremation society was coming to pick him up and the nurses needed to unhook him. At that point I left the hospital, thinking the odd thought that now I didn't have to go back there anymore. I was so exhausted that I surprised myself by being able to fall asleep for a couple of hours. Then, I woke up and it was Monday morning and my new life – one that I never in my wildest dreams expected – would now begin.

Postscript

Right after my husband's death a friend said something to me that turned out to be one of the most beautiful things I had ever heard. Since I have written many World War II and Korean War veterans' stories, it was very meaningful. I had just spent the last years of my life caring for an ill husband, doing everything in my power to help him. This was her response to me:

Mission Accomplished.

Stand Down.

Truly, and only with God's help, I was able to accomplish this mission. Now I could stand down and begin to heal.

PART III:

Discoveries

Three Years On

It has been three years today since I walked out of the hospital room and walked into a new life. Because of the COVID-19 pandemic I was not able to have a service for Bryan. With none of his family in town, where I could have limited invitations to only family, how could I have narrowed an invitation list down to only ten people? I didn't even write an obituary for the local paper in East Texas that might have been interested in publishing it. Because I went through the whole experience of his hospital stays and passing practically alone,* somehow it seemed that his death was a private thing too. That doesn't have to make sense to anyone else – I was a grieving widow.

I might as well insert something here about the pandemic. I tried once to show Bryan photos on my phone of the bare shelves in the grocery store. I don't know if he actually comprehended what I was saying. So, as near as I can tell, he never really experienced any of the results of the pandemic. I was left alone to deal with a world gone crazy. (How very rude of him!) I have had to try to remember that everyone in the whole world was in some way grieving at the same time I was. At a time when I desperately needed everything in the world to run smoothly so I could be comforted, I couldn't go to shops or to eat out. Only two friends came to my house. One brought me a gift basket and one brought takeout and sat and ate it with me. No other friends would hug me – at a time when I could have really used some hugs.* This state of affairs added more trauma onto an already traumatic situation.

Back to the story: that very night at the hospital I had to make a major decision because we had no burial plans. Bryan had never wanted to address this back when he was well, and he had not been able to do so since he became ill. I chose the only option that made sense to me during the pandemic and due to cost – I chose cremation, even though I had never actually considered it for either of us. I know he would have approved because he had become very tight with money over the years and this was definitely the most economical option. I was only going to have a limited amount of life insurance money and I could feel that he would have disapproved of me spending $12,000 or more on a regular burial. Besides, there was no family to go and see a gravesite.

I had to make other big decisions as well. I took the

survivors benefit from Social Security, for example, so I had a way to live, even though that had not been Bryan's and my plan. (Few firms would be interested in hiring a woman in her sixties with little job experience.) I made the decision to sell numerous items to bring in some money. I offered tools and other items in my shed to friends who helped me take care of things around the house: small repairs, a new light fixture, etc., so I didn't have to pay for all the repairs. Most people were very kind to a new widow.

At first I was still extremely angry and hurt. It was actually easier to be angry than to feel the pain of loss. I was also exhausted. Two months passed before I even felt like doing anything. The stress of the abuse and of watching him pass from this earth took its toll on me. Gradually this improved, but still to this day, I don't have the energy I used to have.

Another thing that plagued me during the first months was a recurring nightmare. I would dream that someone met me when I was away from the house. It seemed to be in the parking lot of a business, perhaps a grocery store. A person, who apparently I was supposed to know but actually didn't have a face I recognized, would tell me that they had just seen Bryan and that he would be home soon. They seemed pleased about it. I would wake up screaming, "No! No! No!" I really didn't want the abuse to start back up. I had all I could take of it and now I was free of that, at least. So, normally a widow would dream about her husband coming back and be comforted, but that was not my response.

I love Carol Peters-Tanksley's definition of "normal" when one is grieving:

> Many people wonder if their grief response is normal. If by "normal" you mean your body won't do what it's supposed to, your thoughts don't know where to land, your emotions are difficult or impossible to predict or control, you feel overwhelmed by things that normally would not have bothered you, and your connection with God seems all messed up, then the answer is yes. Messed up, confused, and totally out of sorts is normal…
>
> You may find yourself forgetting simple things, making mistakes your normally wouldn't make, feeling confused, and being unable to concentrate.

That pretty much says how it really feels! You have to understand that no one else feels exactly what you feel, even if they have lost the same family member or friend, and whatever you feel is "normal."

After a few weeks, I wanted to find out more about the puzzle of Bryan's dementia. I had asked the doctor on the floor at the hospital if what he saw on Bryan's CT scan could cause "uncharacteristic behaviors." He replied with certainty that it would cause a loss of inhibition and a loss of impulse control. That was all the information I had to start with, as the doctor was only interested in what was actually causing Bryan's death.

I decided to call our oncologist's office and see if he could look at the CT scan that was taken when Bryan had his motorcycle accident in August of 2017. He called me on the morning of Memorial Day – a dedicated physician! I could tell he was pulling up the scan and it took about three seconds for him to say, "Oh, yes, he had dementia back then." I made some inane comment about everyone losing a few brain cells as they got older and he replied that Bryan's brain "shouldn't look like an eighty-four-year-old!" When he added, "I wonder if this is why he didn't do well after the surgery," I knew he was really seeing a large problem that was obvious on the scan.

Now I had a little more to go on. I began to research through medical journals and various organizations to find out more information about what actually changed in a person's behavior when he or she developed dementia. My findings form the main body of this book. This took up the whole first year of widowhood – a word I absolutely hate, by the way. My life is too valuable to be looked at as a "condition" that I can't fix.

In the second year I realized that even though I had been researching and writing, I had still been in a fog. I didn't feel like myself at all. I now know that it is the brain's way of coping with something it can't understand. My brain thought Bryan would come back home sometime, surely, as he had for forty-three years! Our neurons (a new discovery called object-trace cells) still fire every time we expect our loved one to be there with us. Our brain is assuming they are somewhere else and will be found later. Whole new patterns in the brain have to form for it to incorporate this new reality that our loved one is not going to be there. This leaves the grieving person very disoriented. It's just the way God designed our brains and is not "denial" but something that just takes time to work through.

I am comforted by the fact that people go in and out of denial at different times. Our journey is not linear. Certainly after three years, I know Bryan is gone. However, just a few days ago I had that "it can't be possible" thought again.

We carry our loved ones with us always – encoded in our brain! "It is because your loved one existed that certain neurons fire together and certain proteins are folded in your brain in particular ways. It is because your loved one lived, and because you loved each other, that means when the person is no longer in the outer world, they still physically exist – in the wiring of the neurons of your brain." (*The Grieving Brain*, Mary-Frances O'Connor.)

After the first year, I felt a need to make the house more "mine" than "ours." I took down all the pictures I had on the walls – I never put up family photos, so these were just prints I had purchased over the years – and I bought new prints of beach and ocean scenes. I moved some pieces of furniture around. Anything that would give the place a different look that would more truly express just *my* personality. In the second year I went further, and had the bathrooms refinished. This past year I had a wall filled in so I could arrange the furniture in the library in a better way.

I have perhaps become a "cat lady." My two babies (Jack and Jill, named by Bryan in his last year) have been my constant companions and certainly keep my house lively. I saw a bumper sticker once that had a paw print on it and said, "Who rescued who?" That statement is so correct! I have said more than once that my kittens must secretly be wearing life preservers around their middles so they could rescue me from loneliness. As my understanding of my Heavenly Father has grown, I realize I never feel totally alone. I always feel his presence with me, so there are four of us in the house!

I have appreciated the time I have to study Scripture. I take numerous women's Bible studies at several different churches. This past year I enrolled in Trinity Bible Institute and have now completed my first year. I also take the free courses online from other seminaries, such as Dallas Theological Seminary.

I participate in church activities, an historical group, and meet friends for lunch, among other things. I tell you this because it is important that someone who is grieving not isolate themselves. It is a natural temptation to stay home by yourself and while you don't want to be so busy you don't have time to think, you do need to get out and see others and be part of a community. I have a favorite restaurant where I go in and am greeted by friends. It's been a nice home-away-from-home.

Becoming part of a church home was very important to me, since I really didn't have one anymore due to the complications of Bryan's dementia. I visited several churches, and began attending one regularly. It is a large church, but now I know many people and they know me. It's so nice to know someone cares, and I care about them too.*

Last fall I finished a book for the first time since Bryan's passing. Entitled *Our Heroes Are Not Forgotten Book 6*, it is the story of three women in World War II. It gave me a sense of accomplishment to complete the book because I just hadn't felt like working for so long. I have learned to be more patient with myself and not expect so much so quickly. I have had to give myself permission to grieve and take whatever time I need.

I don't have quite the energy I used to, but I still stay very active with others, because my personality is such that I really need the interaction. Now if only I was that devoted to exercise…well one can't do everything!

Everyone's grieving journey will be different. I don't expect yours to look just like mine and you shouldn't expect that either. Even at the three year point, I still have moments when I look around the house and think – "It's absolutely impossible that this could be true. He CANNOT be dead." Now from my research, I understand why I still have that thought.

Grief never really ends. You will continue to experience small pangs of grief occasionally over your loved one, forever. Before you get too depressed over this, know that your relationship to the feeling that gets triggered in you from time to time changes. It really does. You can start to sense a happy memory behind the pain.

Your path through grief and/or trauma will not linear – you won't just gradually get better every day. You will have ups and downs; do well for a time and then have a setback. It's just the way it is. All I can say is, "Be kind to yourself – give yourself time."

And one other encouraging word:

It WILL get better.

It doesn't hurt as much now.

Honestly.

* One of my sisters was living in town during this time, and she did her very best to try to be there for me and comfort me. Her physical condition made this hard for her, but she went above and beyond to try to help see me through the first year before she had to move away.

How Grief and Trauma Affect Your Brain

I grew to desire to understand why it was taking me so long to recover from Bryan's death and to feel more like myself again. I had foolishly thought it would only take a year or so. That was probably because I was still so angry when he passed. I had to get over the anger first before I could really grieve the good times we had – which was most of our lives, of course.

In this quest to understand, I have seen how our brains react to trauma and to grief and have made a new discovery along the way. I found this all fascinating, and I hope you will enjoy this brief overview.

Trauma is not something everyone grieving will have experienced, but many of us had trauma experiences along with our loved one's passing, or perhaps you experienced trauma in childhood, for example. I discovered a different working definition of trauma in the book, *Triumph Over Trauma*, by Gregory L. Jantz: "Any shocking event that strips a person of his or her fundamental sense of safety." He goes on to say that this need not mean only physical safety, but includes things like the continued viability of our sense of self, of the identity we've built, our reputation, our place in society, and our ability to go on believing that the world is not an openly and aggressively hostile place.

This made me realize how Bryan's behavior during his dementia – when I was not aware of what was going on – was truly a trauma situation. I had invested my life in his and so "the continued viability of my sense of self" was totally affected by his unloving behavior. My reputation as a loving wife and my place in society as a married woman were both threatened. I certainly realized during this time how much these things meant to me. To the point that I was willing to do almost anything to protect them! I now know why I reacted so potentially violently to these threats, due to a new discovery about my own life, which I outline in the next chapter.

Trauma actually makes lasting changes in the function and chemistry of our brains. Bryan was threatening me with bullying and emotional abuse, and seemed to be vaguely threatening me with potential divorce as well, although he didn't take any action on this.

During traumatic stress like this, our brains flip into

survival mode. The amygdala – the part of the brain responsible for our more primitive survival instincts – takes over. It sends out emotional responses, such fear, anger, and sadness. It prompts us to react to danger – the fight, flight, or freeze response. While this is happening, the hippocampus and the prefrontal cortex "go dark." This basically means that you can't think with both the amygdala and the prefrontal cortex at the same time. When I was standing in the hallway of my home and listening to Bryan talking on the phone to the other woman, believe you me I was not thinking with my prefrontal cortex! I was frozen by the door to keep from being seen, like the little rabbits in my backyard look when they realize I am sitting on the deck and can see them. If I'd had the capability, I could have gone in and hurt him in blinding anger and not even realized what I had done until later. That's how frightening it was.

The prefrontal cortex oversees reasoning, problem-solving, and impulse control. This part of your brain helps you process your emotions and regulate your response. So when the amygdala "lights up" and the prefrontal cortex goes "dark," your ability to reason through your emotions and choose how to respond is practically not working at all. You become more fearful, more anxious, and less focused, have memory and sleep problems, and can be fatigued or depressed when your amygdala is overactive. So, trying to *think* and to be *sane* are uphill adventures. Without God watching over me, I could have become a person capable of who knows what type of behavior.

I also discovered why, since Bryan's passing, it seemed that my brain was always working on something in the background and making it hard for me to recall things and think well in the present. I now know that if we are plagued by "why" questions about a traumatic event, our brains work overtime behind the scenes trying to solve the mystery. Even when you don't think you are thinking about the trauma, your brain is thinking about it. No wonder I felt like half my brain wasn't working! It actually wasn't working on what was happening in the present, but was trying to answer my questions about Bryan's hurtful behavior.

I learned that the only way to help this, besides just realizing it, is to try to anchor the trauma to a particular time in the past, so your brain can recognize that it doesn't have to work on this problem anymore. Of course, I was doing the opposite, by still worrying over whether Bryan had stopped loving me. Practicing mindfulness, taking a nature walk, and prayer are good ways to combat this "overtime" work in the brain.

A heightened sense of closeness with God after a

tragedy brings a sense of peace and well-being that would be hard to come by otherwise. This also brings hope – the realization that a new and better life IS possible after trauma and loss. (That's still a little hard to believe.)

As I am fond of saying, God is God and we are not! We don't understand how or why He allows bad things to happen. I believe that everything that happens is not random, but is part of His sovereign plan and that I will understand it in eternity, but now right now. You'd be surprised how comforting that thought is. I can have peace without the need for an explanation. (Although apparently my brain would secretly like an explanation, please!) "Developing a hopeful attitude is far more crucial to wellness than many people recognize." (*Triumph Over Trauma*, Gregory L. Jantz.)

I fell into the trap of several types of negative thinking over the past three years. One psychologists call "counterfactual thinking." These are the "what ifs." Those nasty little thoughts like, "If only I had told her she could never come back to our home…If I had only just kicked her out the door…If only I had changed the locks before Bryan came home that day in November of 2016…would this have made a difference?" At least I don't have those thoughts about his medical care. I know I intentionally did the best I could so as not to have regrets. It's the dementia questions that bother me. If I had known it was dementia and not that he'd stopped loving me, I could have "nipped some of his behavior in the bud," as Barney Fife would say. Unfortunately, this type of thinking is both illogical and unhelpful in my adapting to what has actually happened.

    The mind ruminates when it cannot resolve the discrepancy between its current state and its desired state. Rumination makes you feel as if you are seeking out the truth of the problem, but actually it is prolonging the sad or angry mood you are in, not helping you. The criteria needs to be: is this thought helpful? Rumination can be used as a way to avoid thinking of the painful parts of grief, but it actually takes more effort to avoid those thoughts, and not facing them is not helpful.

    It used to be thought, in our Western world, that having a continuing relationship with the deceased was a bad idea. We worry that someone is stuck in their grief. New science has discovered that it can actually be healthy for some people to have a continuing bond, such as happens in Eastern countries. Ancestor worship is one example, where the beloved relative is remembered and honored and perhaps "consulted" on important family matters. While I wouldn't recommend "worship" by any means, remembering and honoring you loved one, if that fits with your personality, is ALRIGHT. No need to feel you are not grieving well. Some examples might be wearing a child's photo in a locket, naming events in your loved one's honor, and speaking to groups about your loved one, all to keep his or her memory alive. This can make you feel closer to your loved one and that's comforting. This is a way for you to continue to express your love for your loved one. That relationship is no less valuable than it ever was.

Science has much further to go to explain everything that happens in our brains, but what has been discovered is reassuring. The emotions we feel are directly related to God's magnificent design for our brains and thus we can feel and explore and understand ourselves better – and also give ourselves a break when we have strong emotions after trauma and during grief because it's all part of the design.

PART IV:

The Most Important Faith Lessons

The Most Important Faith Lessons I Have Learned

I have had the good fortune to learn from my trauma and loss. This is because I actively sought to learn from these tragic and disturbing experiences. I didn't want what I suffered to be for nothing. I wanted to redeem some of the pain. That's why I wrote this book – it has helped me clarify what happened to me and hopefully my experiences will be a help to others – to you! Even if all you realize is that you are not alone in your pain, then it will have been worth it to write this book.

I learned a surprising lesson in the midst of pain and suffering and loss:

GRATITUDE

is what makes all the difference.

How can this be? How can you express gratitude in the most horrible of times? Why would you even want to try? The answer is: it's the only thing that will help you because it leads you to God and to His precious Son, Jesus.

It takes a while to get to this place, so don't feel badly if you are unable yet to find anything for which to be grateful. What you want to do is to find even the smallest thing for which you can say "thank you" to God: a parking space; a colorful leaf; that the sun is shining; that rain is gently falling; that you can pet your dog or cat's soft fur; that your favorite song is playing; that there is something to eat in your refrigerator, even if you don't feel hungry right now. Start with just basic small things.

Perhaps you have had a faith in God and in His Son, Jesus, for a long time. Perhaps it's just been a part of your life and you have never really had to lean on Jesus or depend on Him. Maybe you've done all right so far. But now, you have hit the most trying time of your life. Maybe, like me, you are unable to depend on the person you were depending on when times were good. Maybe the loved one you are losing or have lost is the one you depended on. Now you have no choice but to find someone else to fill that role.

Now another person (who would also not be perfect) may not be waiting in the wings for you. May I encourage you to turn to Jesus? I have never known a better feeling than the one I feel now at this moment – trusting and depending on the Father God through Him.

He is completely dependable. (Mark 13:31 – "Heaven and earth will pass away, but my words will never pass away.")

He cannot die and leave you. (Deuteronomy 33:27 – "The eternal God is a dwelling place, and underneath are the everlasting arms." Isaiah 40:28 – "The Everlasting God, the Lord, the Creator of the ends of the earth, does not become weary or tired." Psalm 102:12 – "But You, O Lord, abide forever.")

He will never turn His back on you. (Hebrews 13:5 – "Never will I leave you; never will I forsake you.")

He will never make promises that He will not keep. (1 Corinthians 10:13 – "God is faithful." 1 Corinthians 1:9 – "God is faithful, who has called you into fellowship with His Son, Jesus Christ our Lord." 2 Thessalonians 3:3 – "But the Lord is faithful, and He will strengthen you and protect you." 2 Timothy 2:13 – "He remains faithful, for he cannot disown himself.")

He is always watching out for you – 24/7. (Psalms 121:5-8 – "The Lord watches over you – the Lord is your shade at your right hand; the sun will not harm you by day, nor the moon by night. The Lord will keep you from all harm – He will watch over your life; the Lord will watch over your coming and going both now and forevermore." Please note that this does not mean that no things will happen that you will not like; only that He is supervising it all and will make it all turn out to have been for your good.)

He has no agenda except to love you. **He only wants the very best for you**; even if you cannot recognize that what has happened to you is best. (Romans 8:28 – "And we know that in all things God works for the good of those who love Him, who have been called according to His purpose [His will to bring you into His Forever Family]."

He loves you with the purest love imaginable – and He waits for you to come to Him, to share His joy. He offers peace in the midst of pain, hope in the midst of trauma, and joy unspeakable in the future. He sent part of Himself – His Son, Jesus – so that you could be given eternal life. Jesus made the ultimate sacrifice for you in order that you could become part of God's Forever Family. All you have to do is trust Jesus and then you will find that you want to live for Him.

Well, that may be easier said than done for you. How can you trust in Someone you cannot see? How can you know you can depend on God? The answer, for me, is Gratitude. When I begin to think of all the marvelous things God has done, all with the simple desire for sinful human beings to be able to have fellowship with Him, my mind is blown away and my heart is so touched. When I think of all the blessings – the little gifts and treasures I receive each day because I am looking for them – I can hardly believe that the Almighty God of the Universe, Creator of Heaven and Earth, would care about me having a moment of joy today.

You might be thinking, "Well, it's been three years since her husband died, of course she feels better now." And that would be true, but I also remember what it was like on those days when I drove to the hospital to see my husband. I would get to the hospital early, before 6 a.m. so I could get a parking place. On the way, I might see an interestingly shaped tree or a pretty flower in a yard. I would keep driving, but I would spend a moment appreciating what I had seen. I would think, "Even on this miserable day, I just saw something beautiful." This happened day after day.

One morning the woman at the front desk of the hospital asked me how I did it – How did I come early every morning to spend the day with my husband and still be able to smile at her? I had to tell her that I had no strength to do this; it had to be God doing it through me. It seemed to me that He was literally holding me up – like his arms were under my arms, holding me up by the shoulders. There was no way I could be standing up in my own power. I should be collapsed on the floor crying.

Even in the midst of the hardest time of my life, I knew God was with me in the presence of His Son, Jesus. HE IS WITH YOU TOO! Take courage – He will uphold you. (Isaiah 41:10 – "I will strengthen you, I will help you, yes, I will uphold you with My righteous right hand.")

When you learn, as I did, that God the Father is sovereign over everything – meaning He has control over all that happens in this world – and that it is all working for my good, even though I can't understand how it could possibly be for my good – then you have something to be grateful for. Trials like trauma and loss can be what give us unshakeable faith. (John 6:69 – "I believe and confidently trust, and even more, have come to know by personal observation and experience that You are the Son of the Living God.") We know from then on, way down deep inside, that God is FOR us, not against us. This is where the next thing I learned comes in:

SURRENDER

to the will of God in order to find peace.

There is no peace in the idea that all I went through

"just happened" and there's no reason for it. That kind of thinking would make me willing to die with my husband. I have to believe there is a reason and a purpose for what happened to me in the plan of God – in my continuing to live even though my loved one is gone. It can't be just an arbitrary event. There HAS to be meaning in it. That means I need to:

TRUST

God and live in that trust for the rest of my life.

Gratitude is the way I can trust God. Because I know all He has done for me – sending His Son, part of Himself, to die for my sins so I can be part of His Forever Family – and all the little things He does every day to take care of me and show me He loves me – for example, I have a home to live in, a vehicle to drive, cat children to love, enough money to buy food and pay bills, wonderful friends, books to read, and a church to attend – because of all this, I know that God is **trustworthy**. (Isaiah 26:4 – "Trust in the Lord forever, for the Lord God is an everlasting rock." Lamentations 3:22-23 – "The steadfast love of the Lord never ceases; His mercies never come to an end; they are new every morning; great is Your faithfulness." Hebrews 6:18 – "It is impossible for God to lie.")

At this time in my life, I can actually relax into the fact that Someone is watching out for me and I am not alone. I have the best husband ever: Jesus! (Isaiah 54:5-8 – "For your Maker is your husband, The Lord Almighty is His name.")

So I hope it helps you to remember these three things that I have learned:

SURRENDER

to the will of God in order to find peace.

TRUST

God and live in that trust for the rest of your life.

GRATITUDE

is what makes all the difference.

PART IV:

Helps for Coping with Grief and Loss

Some Suggestions for Coping with Grief and Loss

I am still in the process of dealing with my grief. I have learned so much in the last three years about how to progress through grieving. What I expected to take a year – "and I will feel all better" – has turned into a longer journey and I do not know when I will feel that it is "officially" ended. I have learned that one doesn't ever forget the pain of loss; one just learns to live with a residual pain and slowly gain a renewed joy in living. One experiences both pain and joy at the same time: pain that your loved one is no longer with you in person, and joy, as a believer in Jesus, in knowing you will see that loved one again. Joy also begins to grow as you go through new experiences, make new friends, and find renewed purpose in your life.

I cannot forget that Bryan was a part of my whole adult life, nor would I want to forget. He will always be a part of my life, just in a different way. The time that has passed has helped me to be able to remember more of the good part of our life together instead of only the sorrow at the end. That good part was the majority of our time together, after all. I am making the conscious decision not to let dementia take any more away from me by destroying my good memories.

I had a choice to make as a new widow: do I live in anger and bitterness over what happened in the last few years of Bryan's life; or do I turn toward God to find hope and healing? I made the choice to turn toward God and renew my faith in His promises. That choice has made all the difference in the level of peace that is available to me.

Instead of letting anxiety over the unknown future sneak up on me, I spend time each day reading Scriptures that build up my confidence in God's ability to take care of me – to be my husband (Isaiah 54:5). I started a prayer notebook (with ideas from a friend) that I tailored to my personal needs, with sections for veterans and for widows, as well as family and friends, and this has greatly enhanced my prayer life.

These things give meaning and purpose to my life. When a woman loses her husband, her main job – that of wife – is over and it is a challenge to find a new reason to get up each day.

Three major resources have helped me on my

journey in addition to leaning on God: my Hospice counselor, the *Restored* workbook, and GriefShare. I worked with a Hospice bereavement counselor during the first thirteen months after my loss and this made my transition easier. As the reader can recognize, I had a great deal of pain and hurt to work through and I considered having the professional help to be a must. The stress of these last few years has been tremendous and in the first couple of months I realized how exhausted I really was. I am still learning to be kind to myself, after those years of being poorly treated and feeling unloved. Don't be hesitant about receiving professional help to work through your loss.

The workbook, *Restored: A Self-paced Grief Workbook for You Journey From Loss to Life*, by Marilyn Willis, MA, LPCC, NCC, was a pleasant surprise. I found it online by "chance." As the title suggests, you work through the book on your own, but she does have other resources available. Her approach, after counseling many grieving families, is found in five principles: 1. Reestablish Order, 2. Reset Expectations, 3. Remember Your Loved One, 4. Renew Identity, and 5. Restore Life After Loss. I have found her ideas to be quite helpful and felt that I had more understanding of the grieving process as I have completed each exercise. Ms. Willis does have a Christian background and includes some scriptures. I highly recommend this tool.

GriefShare, from Church Initiative, has been a wonderful resource. Attending a group and hearing the stories of others who are grieving is more helpful than you realize it could be. The workbook and videos are scripture-based and comprehensive, with thirteen sessions dealing with topics such as, "Is This Normal?"; how grief affects your other relationships; handling anger and guilt; feeling stuck; coping skills; looking forward to heaven; and "What Do I Live for Now?" The six goals for the grief journey are expressed as: 1. Acceptance, 2. Turn to God, 3. Express Emotions, 4. Establish a New Identity, 5. Moving Forward, and 6. Store Memories.

I cannot recommend these three resources highly enough. Each has made such a difference in my life. The best decision I have made, though, it to more completely surrender my life to God. Depending on him lifts the burden of a frightening future off my shoulders and gives me confidence that I am cared for in his arms.

Some Immediate Help

Everyone will mourn a loss at some time in their lives. If you are experiencing such a time right now, here is some immediate help for you:

Melinda Smith, M.A., Lawrence Robinson, and Jeanne Segal, Ph.D. share help for those who grieve, especially in reminding the griever that each person is an individual and there is no one "right" way to express grief:

Grief is a natural response to loss. It's the emotional suffering you feel when something or someone you love is taken away. Often, the pain of loss can feel overwhelming. You may experience all kinds of difficult and unexpected emotions, from shock or anger to disbelief, guilt, and profound sadness. The pain of grief can also disrupt your physical health, making it difficult to sleep, eat, or even think straight. These are normal reactions to loss—and the more significant the loss, the more intense your grief will be.

The authors also remind us that there are many times of grief in our lives, not only at the death of a loved one, including a divorce or relationship breakup; loss of health; losing a job; loss of financial stability; a miscarriage; retirement; death of a pet; loss of a cherished dream; a loved one's serious illness; loss of a friendship; and a loss of safety after a trauma. All of these occurrences can result in grieving symptoms. "Whatever your loss, it's personal to you, so don't feel ashamed about how you feel, or believe that it's somehow only appropriate to grieve for certain things. If the person, animal, relationship, or situation was significant to you, it's normal to grieve the loss you're experiencing."

It is helpful to know that there is no "normal" timetable for grieving. Some people feel better sooner than others. The one thing that doesn't work is to try to avoid grieving: "Trying to ignore your pain or keep it from surfacing will only make it worse in the long run. For real healing, it is necessary to face your grief and actively deal with it."

Some common feelings you may experience during the grieving period include (but not in any particular order):

1. Denial: "This can't be happening to me."
2. Anger: "Why is this happening? Who is to blame?"
3. Bargaining: "Make this not happen, and in return I will _____."
4. Depression: "I'm too sad to do anything."
5. Acceptance: "I'm at peace with what happened."

You don't have to "be strong" in the face of loss. Even though Vera said that, "I tried to be submissive to God's will – to be brave and strong. The harder I tried, the more God helped me," it is obvious that she did not rely solely on her own strength to do so. She cooperated with God in the process. "Feeling sad, frightened, or lonely is a normal reaction to loss. Crying doesn't mean you are weak. You don't need to 'protect' your family or friends by putting on a brave front. Showing your true feelings can help them and you."

"There are ways to help cope with the pain, come to terms with your grief, and eventually, find a way to pick up the pieces and move on with your life." The authors suggest these steps to help deal with the grieving process:

1. Acknowledge your pain.

2. Accept that grief can trigger many different and unexpected emotions.
3. Understand that your grieving process will be unique to you.
4. Seek out face-to-face support from people who care about you.
5. Support yourself emotionally by taking care of yourself physically.
6. Recognize the difference between grief and depression.

Just as Vera's notes suggest, one experiences ups and downs in the grieving process:

> We might think of the grieving process as a roller coaster, full of ups and downs, highs and lows. Like many roller coasters, the ride tends to be rougher in the beginning; the lows may be deeper and longer. The difficult periods should become less intense and shorter as time goes by, but it takes time to work through a loss. Even years after a loss, especially at special events such as a family wedding or the birth of a child, we may still experience a strong sense of grief. (Hospice Foundation of America.)

Some of the emotional symptoms of grief shared by the authors (these can come in any order) include:

1. **Shock and disbelief**

After a loss, it can be hard to accept what happened. You may feel numb, have trouble believing that the loss really happened, or even deny the truth. (Remember that Vera expressed this very feeling while she was still at John Sealy Hospital.) If someone you love has died, you may keep expecting them to show up, even though you know they're gone. (I still have this experience occasionally even three years later.)

2. **Sadness**

Profound sadness is probably the most universally experienced symptom of grief. You may have feelings of emptiness, despair, yearning, or deep loneliness. You may also cry a lot or feel emotionally unstable.

3. **Guilt**

You may regret or feel guilty about things you did or didn't say or do. You may also feel guilty about certain feelings (e.g. feeling relieved when the person died after a long, difficult illness). After a death, you may even feel guilty for not doing something to prevent the death, even if there was nothing more you could have done. This blame you put on yourself is terribly unfair and unproductive.

4. Anger

Even if the loss was nobody's fault, you may feel angry and resentful. If you lost a loved one, you may be angry with yourself, God, the doctors, or even the person who died for abandoning you. You may feel the need to blame someone for the injustice that was done to you.

5. Fear

A significant loss can trigger a host of worries. You may feel anxious, helpless, or insecure. You may even have panic attacks. The death of a loved one can trigger fears about your own mortality, of facing life without that person, or the responsibilities you now face alone.

These emotional symptoms can be difficult to deal with. You might also experience physical symptoms such as fatigue, nausea, lowered immunity, weight loss or weight gain, aches and pains, or insomnia. "When you're grieving, it's more important than ever to take care of yourself. The stress of a major loss can quickly deplete your energy and emotional reserves."

The authors (and other sources I have read)

suggest the following types of self-care for the grieving person:

1. **Face your feelings.**

You can try to suppress your grief, but you can't avoid it forever. In order to heal, you have to acknowledge the pain. Trying to avoid feelings of sadness and loss only prolongs the grieving process.

2. **Express your feelings in a tangible way.**

Write about your loss in a journal. If you've lost a loved one, write a letter saying the things you never got to say; make a scrapbook or photo album celebrating the person's life; or get involved in a cause or organization that was important to your loved one.

3. **Try to maintain your hobbies and interests.**

There's comfort in routine and getting back to the activities that bring you joy and connect you closer to others can help you come to terms with your loss and aid the grieving process.

4. **Don't let anyone tell you how to feel.**

Each person's grief journey is unique. Don't tell yourself how to feel either. Your grief is your own, and no one else can tell you when it's time to "move on" or "get over it." Let yourself feel whatever you feel without embarrassment or judgment.

5. **Plan ahead for "triggers."**
Anniversaries, holidays, and milestones can reawaken memories and feelings. Be prepared for an emotional wallop, and know that it's completely normal. If you're sharing a holiday or lifecycle event with other relatives, talk to them ahead of time about their expectations and agree on strategies to honor the person you loved.

6. **Look after your physical health**.
The mind and body are connected. When you feel healthy physically, you'll be better able to cope emotionally.

7. **Seek professional help.**
You may need help to work through any issues you might have.

I know wish you well in healing from your grief and once again facing life with joy.

Some Comforting Scriptures

Psalm 147:3

He heals the brokenhearted and binds up their wounds.

Psalm 61:1-2

Hear my cry, O God; listen to my prayer. From the ends of the earth I call to you, I call as my heart grows faint; lead me to the rock that is higher than I.

Isaiah 41:10

So do not fear, for I am with you; do not be dismayed, for I am your God. I will strengthen you and help you; I will uphold you with my righteous right hand.

Psalm 4:8

In peace I will lie down and sleep, for you alone, Lord, make me dwell in safety.

John 16:33

I have told you these things, so that in me you may have peace. In this world you will have trouble. But take heart! I have overcome the world.

Psalm 30:5b

Weeping may stay for the night, but rejoicing comes in the morning.

2 Corinthians 12:9

My grace is sufficient for you, for my power is made perfect in weakness.

Psalm 3:3

But you, Lord, are a shield around me, my glory, the One who lifts my head high.

Philippians 4:6-7

Do not be anxious about anything, but in everything, by prayer and petition, with thanksgiving, present your requests to God. And the peace of God, which transcends all understanding, will guard your hearts and your minds in Christ Jesus.

Lamentations 3 22-23

Because of the Lord's great love we are not consumed, for his compassions never fail. They are new every morning; great is your faithfulness.

John 14:1-3

Do not let your hearts be troubled. You believe in God[a]; believe also in me. 2 My Father's house has many rooms; if that were not so, would I have told you that I am going there to prepare a place for you? 3 And if I go and prepare a place for you, I will come back and take you to be with me that you also may be where I am.

Hebrews 13:5

I will never leave you nor forsake you.

Matthew 11:28-29

Come to me, all you who are weary and burdened, and I will give you rest. Take my yoke upon you and learn from me, for I am gentle and humble in heart, and you will find rest for your souls.

Proverbs 3:5-6

Trust in the LORD with all your heart and lean not on your own understanding; in all your ways submit to him, and he will make your paths straight.

Psalm 55:22

Cast your cares on the Lord and he will sustain you; he will never let the righteous be shaken.

Psalm 46:1

God is our refuge and strength, an ever-present help in trouble.

1 Peter 5:7

Cast all your anxiety on him because he cares for you.

John 14:27

Peace I leave with you; my peace I give you. I do not give to you as the world gives. Do not let your hearts be troubled and do not be afraid.

Psalm 23

The Lord is my shepherd, I lack nothing. He makes me lie down in green pastures, he leads me beside quiet waters, he refreshes my soul. He guides me along the right paths for his name's sake. Even though I walk through the darkest valley, I will fear no evil, for you are with me; your rod and your staff, they comfort me. You prepare a table before me in the presence of my enemies. You anoint my head with oil; my cup overflows. Surely your goodness and love will follow me all the days of my life, and I will dwell in the house of the Lord forever.

Some Journaling Prompts

Using journaling as a healing tool can help you identify your emotions, process unpleasant memories, and help you come to terms with your loss and/or trauma. In a way, this book is also my journal.

For Loss

(Shared from *The Christian's Journey Through Grief* by Carol Peters-Tanksley.)

1. What did your loved one mean to you? What was special about the person as an individual?

2. What do you miss right now about your loved one?

3. What would you like to tell your loved one if you could do so?

4. What reminded you of your loved one today? How did it feel?

5. What worries you about the future? What challenges are you facing as a result of your loved one's death?

6. What about your loved one's life do you want to carry with you into the future?

7. How did your loved one impact who you are as a person?

8. Has God been saying anything to you through your grief journey?

For Trauma

(Shared from Swarnakshi Sharma at *Calm Sage*)

1. Write about your safe space including what it means to you and how you created it.

2. List at least five positive things the trauma has had on your life.

3. Write about what forgiveness means to you.

4. Write a letter to yourself (it could be your older self, the current you, or your younger self).

5. Write about a trauma response that you're currently processing and how it affects your life.

6. Write about the challenges you faced today and how you overcame them.

7. Write about at least one thing you learned today and would not want to forget.

8. Write about the symptoms you experienced today and how you managed them.

9. Write about how you can show yourself the same understanding, compassion, and kindness as you would a loved one.

10. Write about when you feel the most at peace.

11. Write about the emotions from the past you're still holding on to.

12. Write about the ways your trauma has impacted your behavior and thinking process.

13. Write about the ways you've grown from your trauma.

14. Write about if and when you've downplayed your traumatic experiences. Why?

15. Do you hold negative feelings toward the person or event that caused the trauma? Why?

16. Write about the ways you've made progress and healed from your trauma.

17. Write about how you cope with uncomfortable memories, emotions, and thoughts.

18. Write about the ways you've persevered despite the trauma you've experienced.

Books Cited

Doctor, Courtney. *In View of God's Mercies - Bible Study Book with Video Access: The Gift of the Gospel in Romans*. Lifeway Press, February 2022.

Jantz, Gregory L., Ph.D. *Triumph Over Trauma*. Fleming H. Revell Company, March 2023.

O'Connor, Mary-Frances. *The Grieving Brain: New Discoveries about Love, Loss, and Learning*. HarperOne, New York, NY, 2022.

Peters-Tanksley, Carol. *The Christian's Journey Through Grief: How to Walk Through the Valley With Hope*. Charisma House, May 7th 2019.

About the Author

Kathleen Shelby Boyett is an International Author and Historian who specializes in writing veterans' stories. Her wish is that "no veteran will feel forgotten." She also assists other clients in writing their memoirs. Ms. Boyett is a former Board Member of the North Carolina Military Veterans Hall of Fame, a supporter of the Military Order of the Purple Heart, a member of the Metrolina Wing of the 8th Air Force, and the National Society Daughters of the American Revolution. She attends many veterans' coffees, takes veterans to lunch, speaks to senior and veterans' groups, and hosts the Annual Gathering of Heroes each year. Ms. Boyett is the author of over twenty books about American History. Her books are sold in the gift shops of historical sites and museums, as well as online.

Made in the USA
Columbia, SC
23 September 2023

23242429R00130